God Who?
From Stranger to Superhero

*A Woman's Journey through Family,
Failure and Faith*

Merideth Parrish

God Who? From Stranger to Superhero

Booktango books may be ordered through booksellers or by contacting:

Booktango
1663 Liberty Drive
Bloomington, IN 47403
www.booktango.com
877-445-8822

ISBN: 978-1-4689-3965-1 (ebook)

Contents

Dedication

To Mother, Christine, Ruby, Jeanne and Aldoria—whose names are

love, peace, patience, kindness and self-control.

Thank you for enabling me to answer the question, "God Who?"

Let Us Pray

Lord, so many times in life we delve into unchartered waters—some filled with scary creatures, unknown obstacles and unforeseen pains. But because you are our Father, you've promised to never leave nor forsake us, no matter what lies ahead.

Help us to remember that we are your children, and have been equipped with your Holy Spirit, your Holy Word, and a supernatural sense of authority, power and sound mind—all gifts given by you, because you love us. If we keep our hands in yours, we will not fall, we cannot fail.

If we are unsure of what it means to trust you wholly and completely, increase our faith daily. Give us reminders however you see fit—through scriptures, gentle words of encouragement from friends, or perhaps in the most unexpected times, trials and places.

Thank you for loving us more than we could possibly love ourselves. We are excited about the possibilities and brighter days that lie ahead as we learn to love, trust, and embrace you more. Amen

Chapter 1

Life as a Continuum: Knowledge, Truth and Honesty

Everyone should do it. Reflect on it, cry at the exposure of it, laugh at the absurdity of it and celebrate the joy of going through it. It is your story, your life's continuum. This is mine.

While my life is not built on egregious lies and false faces, it is one that harbors hidden treasures, painful secrets, dark shadows and indescribable joys. Conditions a relationship with Jesus Christ, over time has begun to suppress and more importantly to heal. I am Merideth. As a black woman having lived just thirty-two years of life, I have encountered and survived experiences—some, no one should and others, people would not believe. Everything about my upbringing had "success story" written all over it—adopted at birth, raised in a loving Christian home, schooled at some of the finest Christian establishments in the Midwest and reared around the spirit-filled saints of the Church of Christ Holiness. One would think my redemption story would be fail-proof. The roadmap I would create for my adolescent life would become tattered, soiled and skewed. But Christ's blueprint was never flawed; it would withstand even the testiest of navigators and the most dangerous of detours.

At some point in our lives, we've all come across some very personal and emotional stories describing how a young man or a young girl was perhaps abused, neglected or misguided as a child, rebelled in attempts to find a source of love and comfort, and wandered aimlessly to amass a sense of identity and belonging. Somewhere in the midst of wandering a beacon of hope—an "ah ha" moment occurs and a superstar emerges; salvation has come. For Christians this story has far greater meaning than perhaps we realize. Not only do these stories characterize the raw and imperfect matter of which man is made, but they speak wholly and powerfully to the awesome greatness and mercy of our God. When everything about our history, our carnal and corrupt past speaks destruction and defeat, the journey reveals the hope and healing that comes from a Savior. As Christians, we call this our testimony. We can relate to similar stories and each other because we know how the story ends.

For those who have never encountered Jesus or have yet to become members of Christ's family, there is little connection with this end, but there is an understanding of the journey. As people—earth's people, we hurt the same. We've been angered, abused, neglected, mistreated and abandoned. We've watched as people suffer and those we love have taken their final breaths. It is for you who are going through the journey that I offer my story; a true and sobering tale that is the journey of my life. May you come to see through its weavings and unexpected miracles, the hope and boundless possibilities that exist when Jesus Christ *is* your end.

What makes this story conceivably, unlike any other "journeys" you've read? Mine, like most stories is incomplete. While I have come to a deep and sensational love for Jesus Christ just by accepting Him as my Lord and Savior, every day I struggle with doubt, uncertainties, addictions and temptations. As I have faced this journey, I have discovered that true wisdom—Godly wisdom— is found along a continuum of knowledge, truth, and honesty.

Knowledge is the foundation of my faith, the Biblical principles and truths God established to help me fight those daily struggles. These truths are found in versus like Matthew 19:26 which says ". . . with God all things are possible" and Romans 8:37-39 that confirms ". . . we are more than conquerors through (Jesus) who loved us . . . . [and] nothing will be able to separate us from the love of God that is in Christ Jesus our Lord."

Truth is what is confirmed to be real and undisputable. It is an undisputable fact for example, that one day we all will die. We will leave our bodies to emerge into our eternal dwelling place. Eternity my friends, is also very real. As humans born into sin, we were never intended to dwell in an earthly state, to thrive in fleshly human form forever. We simply cannot; our redemption is found in the restoration that comes in our reunion with Jesus Christ, a heavenly post-mortal reunion. As a child, this truth terrified me greatly. Over time however, l learned Jesus was also very clear about truth—in His actions, in His teachings and through His word, the Bible. Everything He said and did was irrefutable and undoubtedly reliable.

Why Jesus? Simply put, without Him eternity isn't possible. Jesus and everything about Him is holy, pure and perfect. If we look at the world around us—the pain, disease and violence that comprise our earthly journey—humans are imperfect. By ourselves, we are unable to attain the eternal purity and unending bliss that awaits in heaven. So how do we get there? How do we bridge the gap between the frightening thought of death and a blissful, eternal home in paradise? In today's world, perception, truth and reality are virtually synonymous. What we perceive is what is true. If we perceive we have a need, we acknowledge a solution is required—hence the billion dollar tagline *there's an app for that*. As humans, we needed a Savior. Jesus was and still is the app for that. His resolve is simple, three truths and one very clear solution.

Truth: We Need a Savior (The Problem)
For all have sinned and fall short of the Glory of God (Romans 3:23)
And he said: "I tell you the truth, unless you change . . . you will never enter the kingdom of heaven. (Matthew 18:3)

Truth: God Sent Us a Savior (The Ah-Ha moment!)
For God so loved the world that he gave his one and only Son, that whoever believes in him shall not perish but have eternal life (John 3:16)

Truth: Salvation is Simple (The Solution, Confess and Believe)
. . . If you confess with your mouth, "Jesus is Lord," and believe in your heart that God raised him from the dead, you will be saved. (Romans 10:9)

God, in an act of indescribable love and grace sent his son Jesus to earth to die in our place. Man, by nature is sinful. By default, this disposition means we cannot experience eternal life on our own and will not in this present life. As God's only son, Jesus as pure and was without sin. He was the perfection of God embodied in the fleshly form of man. His death not only paid our ransom—exchanging his life for our own, but undoubtedly, Jesus' sacrifice tore the veil separating man from God. Because of Jesus, we have inherited the right to live again.

In John 14:2-3 after Jesus was crucified and rose from the grave defeating sin and death, He made a promise to his children here on earth, one that would seal the legitimacy of our faith. He said,

> *In my Father's house are many rooms (mansions); if it were not so,*
> *I would have told you. I am going there to prepare a place for you.*
> *And if I go and prepare a place for you, I will come back and take*
> *you to be with me that you also may be where I am.*

It is this truth that affirms why I am a Christian, a believer in Jesus and a lover of everything He has to offer. His gift of salvation is free to anyone who seeks it, requiring only that we 1) confess our sinful nature; 2) believe He is the true and solitary being able to forgive our sins through his death and resurrection; 3) and pledge our lives to being His followers, sharing and living out the virtues His holiness represents. The latter of these three conditions is what has birthed this story. Anyone can *confess* and even *believe*. However, it is in the lives we live, particularly when no one is watching, we find perhaps the most important and revealing part of our life's continuum—our honesty.

This journey, my story, reveals me—honestly. As a professional, a friend, a family member and even a church-goer, I have learned to portray a life that is necessary. It's quite scary actually, to think I have a work face, a mom face, a wife face, a kid's school face and yes—my congregational face. I have come to find as followers of Jesus Christ, when we transition through a continuum of wisdom—gaining knowledge and affirming our Biblical truths, we are quick to erase and sometimes wholly forget the honesty of who we once were; and for some of us, remain to be. This story won't reveal my life and its lies, but it will take you through the journey. While riddled with instances of youthful missteps, parenting mistakes and marital faux pas you will find the underlying theme of victory in each tale. It is not my victory mind you, it is a testament of God's mercy and what is possible when you allow yourself to move along the continuum God desires for your life, a *continuum of Christian character.*

Why A Continuum?

When I started the daunting task of documenting my reunification with Christ (this will soon make sense), it was early one Thursday morning in October, 2012-1:00 a.m. to be exact. I didn't know why I was writing, I just was. I loved to write. I still do. With a professional career in communications, there isn't a time when I'm not overflowing with thoughts, ideas and . . . songs. Only second to my love of God and family is my love of music; and not just any music—worship songs, melodies of praise. I was a self-proclaimed singer/songwriter with no formal training nor access to studio production. Leading worship, particularly youth worship at my local church was my passion. I prayed and at times found myself begging God to open doors for my music ministry to erupt. Many prayers, several songs, no eruption; so that Thursday morning I wrote.

As I started to put key strokes to paper my goal was to capture my journey, my life's story for my children. There was so much they didn't know about me—details and stories of God's heroism that I no doubt would botch with bad story telling—that I wanted them to know. I needed them to grasp not how amazing their mother was but how awesome the God we serve is and has been, for generations long before their time. I desired for them to understand the depth and power of their heritage as children and heirs of Christ. When everything around them speaks of hopelessness and uncertainty, God is a tried and true foundation.

Those key strokes soon turned into tears, later into songs, memories that tapered off into whispered sighs, "my God . . . how did we ever survive," and finally a prayer of praise. As I crafted the introduction I asked God, "Why continuum? That's not catchy, it's far from meaningful—what am I supposed to do with that?" With just me, the typing of my HP keyboard and the steady humming of the refrigerator God simply whispered, "Yes, continuum—this is your continuum . . . keep writing." So I wrote.

By definition the term "continuum" indicates a gradual transition or progression from one condition to a different condition. In practical terms it signifies evolution—a mechanism by which change is accomplished. My continuum is my journey. In it is revealed the honesty that may surprise some, offend others, and inspire those in search of life's victorious ending. It describes a process through which I have come to the knowledge of who God is, accepted the truth of why God is, and am now dealing with the daily challenge of embracing all that Christian faith implies—responsibility, authenticity, accountability and honesty.

Although I acknowledged Jesus as my Savior almost twenty years ago, I find myself struggling still to understand just who God is. I'm confident I owe Him my time, my devotion, my life's pursuit, but why? Some days, when I feel desperation taking away my very breath and all remaining ounces of hope, I mutter a small, "How, how can I praise you God?" And then there are other days still I ask the question, "God who?" almost taunting Him to answer me in a thunderous roar. It is in these times I wish He would just descend from the sky—to rescue me, answer me, heck—even chastise me, but I need to feel Him, I want to see Him, I long to believe He really cares.

The truth—our time on earth is limited. People are hurting, suffering and dying—all the while, looking for a lifeline. When we accept the continuum God has ordained for our lives—the process by which God desires to build, grow and sustain us as Christ followers, God slowly and gently reveals how hope, forgiveness and healing are possible. There isn't one who is ineligible or unworthy of the Savior's love.

It is my hope, no matter who you are or where you find yourself to be at this very moment in your life's story, you use my journey to frame your own continuum and you discover the answer—a personal and convincing answer to the question, "God Who?" It is my prayer this story reveals a situation, a loved one or even an addiction that seems impossible to mitigate. And in that moment you realize your continuum is a progression to the end—the final goal toward which you should strive, and that you marvel in the discovery of life's vehicle who is Jesus Christ, the one who will carry you and build your faith as you walk hand in hand with Him.

As you travel along this journey with me, embrace the victories, the miracles and the Godly interventions that occur often times without human orchestration. God knew the footprint of my continuum—how long it would be, how far from the center line I would stray, and the mechanisms required to bring me back. The same God who covered and carried me is waiting for you.

Ready? Here we go.

Chapter 2

She, She and Me

B is for Betty and for brave. That's my mother, a brave woman, she always has been. Frequently soft spoken and undaunted by life's quick and easy pleasures, Betty is a hard worker who has pursued and persevered her entire life. When breast cancer threatened to steal her joy and her very life, she prayed and believed God for its removal, never to return. It returned, but again she prayed. That was just Betty's way—praying, believing and then praying some more.

Born in the small rural town of Winnsboro, Louisiana, mother saw very humble beginnings which included a small three bedroom home shared by five brothers and two sisters. As a child mother was raised by two parents—Madere, *pronounced mah-dear* (a popular and endearing term for black mothers and grandmothers, primarily used in the south) and her father, Carey.

Madere or my *Gran* as I would call her, was a woman of small stature who packed a powerful posture. Her life was her testimony. Her strength and her might demonstrated both in words and in deeds, all nestled behind her crème colored skin and her warm gentle smile. Her husband Carey spent the majority of his life with one clear designation, the provider. He was the breadwinner of the family which made him the authoritarian. He embodied the role in every sense of the word.

He was the disciplinarian, an ominous figure standing a frightening six foot three inches tall *(frightening at least for a small child in the 1940's)* and was known by his children as Dad. He was the—didn't talk much, but when he spoke you listened—Dad. I knew Carey as Papa. I only saw him a few times, perhaps more than I can remember. Visits to their quaint raised ranch in Winnsboro were exciting. The fourteen-hour drive, ice cream stops along the way and pulling into the car port at 1902 Harvard Street just a minute before midnight made me feel like gold. I was loved by my Gran and my Papa.

Toward the end of his life when Carey became a Christian, his demeanor and his very image changed. The man who at one time refused to grace a dance recital, a high school football game and on some nights the dining room table, was forever changed. Of the eight children, some came to know and love this Carey. Others were long gone from the humble homestead and would never have the joy.

My mother was raised by parents who feared God, particularly Gran. Gran spent most of her life as a devoted teacher. Weekdays were spent teaching grammar and arithmetic at the schoolhouse while Sundays were reserved for Bible class at the church. Gran loved being a Sunday school teacher where her timid and quiet nature was transformed by her passionate spirit and her unwavering love for God. I can recall countless stories my mother would tell about Gran. She would describe how Gran raised eight children practically on her own, but all the while never mumbled a groan or complaint. She would say, "my mother loved her children, she loved us so," and would beam with smiles of joy as she described the home-cooked meals, heavenly smells of sweet potato pie and the serenade of songs from the *His Fullness* hymnal that poured from their overcrowded kitchen.

Gran was the flagstaff, the foundation of the family's faith while Carey was the backbone keeping them all upright. Together, mother and father instilled a strong sense of discipline in each child, one that included a love of family, a pursuit of knowledge through education, and the possibility of something greater than what lie in the 318 square miles of Winnsboro. These principles, so strong and rich would be the foundation of their strength and character as human beings.

Indeed, my mother is a fascinating woman and when I think about who she is, the values she instilled in me, I think about from whence she came. And frankly, it all makes sense. She emerged from a home whose cornerstone was Jesus Christ. While her parents would be spiritually divided for most of her childhood, it was Gran—the tears, her gentle hands and the compassion of a praying mother that sustained Jesus as the base. He would be the head until

Carey's appointed time. Jesus would be the center of every book read, every discussion had, every meal consumed.

Gran, my Gran was an amazing woman. I could write a novel solely dedicated to lauding her great wisdom, her courage, her stories of survival and her voice—oh, the songs she used to sing. When I think of Gran, I see my mother and I know full well how she became the miraculous woman she is; a brave, inspiring woman of God—because of my Gran.

On many occasions, mother and I have reflected on memories and everything that was Carey Neal. In her early days, she would describe her father in relation to the fear he produced among his children. It certainly wasn't an abusive-type fear, but a fear of the belt, his thunderesque voice bellowing through the long dark corridor when beds were found unmade and clothes lay strewn about the floor. Mother knew the consequences if work were left undone. Later in life she learned to appreciate and admire who her father was and why he did the things he did. Fear became appreciation, appreciation would grow to love. Looking back as an adult, mother realized Carey's action were characteristic of who he was in relation to his continuum. Initially perhaps, his gruff exterior and lack of affection were a result of *his* upbringing, a time in which men were not encouraged to love and to show love. Men weren't sensitive creatures; they were governing authorities to be respected—the breadwinner, the strongman, the firm hand.

When I consider this relationship of father and daughter—Carey and Betty, it so clearly equates to the relationship I have built with *my father*, Jesus Christ. When I first became a Christian, it truly was out of fear. My timid and untimely walk to the altar transpired out of sheer admiration for this ominously powerful being who commanded the seas, crippled nations and orchestrated the very earth into being. He was this big, global deity I didn't know personally and was convinced despite what anyone or anything said, I didn't *stand* a chance to know because I was me, little ol' sinful me. Furthermore, did I even want to know this God? The thought of what He could do to me made me shutter like a worm whose hiding spot had been unearthed. I feared the powerful and matchless wrath of a very big God.

In my mind though, there were conflicts I couldn't shake. I knew certain things to be true. I knew if one sinned, lived and remained living a life impenitently of sin, the ultimate consequence was death (*Romans 6:23*). I didn't want to die. I wasn't quite sure where I would go, so I knew I wasn't ready to die. I also knew without a savior, more importantly—without Jesus Christ, there was no possibility of seeing heaven's gates; no chance of living forever. I *wanted* to live forever. The very thought of being loved, experiencing love and being surrounded by people who loved me forever and ever was unfathomable. I knew a lot of things *about* God, but I didn't *know* God.

Bottom line, it was my fear of God that drove me to a desire and essentially an intrigue to become saved. Over time and experience, as I moved along my continuum, I realized God was so much more than a God to be feared. Proverbs 9:10 describes how the fear of the Lord is the beginning of wisdom. It wasn't wrong to fear God; it was simply a natural beginning to my Christian continuum. The wisdom acquired through this initial fear would become the knowledge base in which I would learn to long for God. It would be this fear that would lead me to search for answers and to truly understand what and why I believe in Jesus Christ.

It's no wonder, true knowledge is power. Once I came into the knowledge of Jesus, the relationship He and I formed as father and daughter—I became empowered to go much farther beyond fear. With knowledge and understanding came appreciation: a deep gratitude of who God is, *why* He is and what He actually meant to me as an individual. As I matured in my relationship with God, all the while moving along my continuum, I would discover He was no longer that big, ominous figured to be feared—one I couldn't possibly comprehend. Instead, He would walk with me and become a part of me. Just as Carey became father for Betty.

When I think of my continuum and my quest to understand who God is, I go back to the beginning—just mother and me. Mother's commitment was indescribable. From the time we became a pair, she did everything she could to ensure my life, an unexpected opportunity, was spared. Our union was destined long before I was conceived; another amazing example of God's perfection in our weakness and in the most unpredictable of times. The story of my adoption is one of pure joy, an emotional tale with perhaps a fairytale ending. As a child though, I didn't understand it. I questioned the integrity behind it. I simply couldn't fathom why a mother would give her child away. Perhaps it was immaturity, a lack of knowledge and understanding of unseen peripheral issues. But God knew; He had greater foresight, a much wiser plan.

E is for Evelyn, which in Hebrew means *life*. Evelyn was the giver of my life, the biological mother who loved me undeniably from the time I graced her womb. Her love was a selfless love. She too is an amazing woman, one of remarkable strength, courage and character. Her stories, her life experiences moved her along a continuum of discovery and faith. Her past once bore periods of pain and destruction. She is a survivor, a victor who has since transformed into a radical for Christ. Today she is an ambassador who has experienced first-hand, the saving power of Jesus.

In the midst of her journey she would be abused, abandoned and would bear a child. But it was not her child, nor was it her will, but it would be God's plan she would be called to follow. I imagine at one point she felt like Abraham, who was instructed to sacrifice his first born out of obedience and as a demonstration of his unwavering faith in God. Abraham would obey, his son would be spared, and his physical and spiritual life forever to prosper. Even though she would obey, I can only imagine that final conversation with God—tearfully, heart heavy, almost inaudibly uttering the words, "Why God?" But in blind faith, she heeded the Lord's instructions.

Six weeks is such a short time for a new mother. Her body is changing, baby refuses to sleep, emotions run high. But at six weeks, Evelyn was composed. She was nervous, perhaps a bit unsettled, but she was calm if only for those brief, vital moments. With palms sweating and heart trembling, she called. She called her sister, Betty. With as few words as possible she uttered, "You need to come now . . . it's time. You need to take her before I can't let her go."

More than 300 miles away, the voice on the other end of the phone was frozen by the words she heard. She had planned, she had prayed, yet still she sat frozen; for she too was deep in the throes of her own troubled season. Trapped in a relationship riddled with physical and verbal assaults, she would cry out to God only a few days before, "Lord, if you help me get out of this, I will serve you faithfully. I will worship you forever. I will be your disciple."

I've asked my mother Betty to tell me the story time and time again. It reminds me just how much I was loved by those women and how much God loved those women He rescued that day. I would say to her, "Mom, tell me again . . . how did it happen." Intently I would drill her to see if the story ever changed. "Did you really feel trapped? You really couldn't escape?" I asked skeptically. She would reply, "I thought that man was going to kill me. He threatened me; he said he'd kill me if I ever left." My mother did not lie. From that moment I knew I was her miracle.

Days later after pleading with God, He answered. When she received the phone call from Evelyn, she knew the Lord was orchestrating divine intervention for both she and her sister. He had heard their collective pleas—He was sending a lifeline.

Betty boarded a plane headed for Hope, Arkansas where I was waiting. Aunt would become mother and mother would become aunt.

I don't know many details of the exchange. I never ask. I can only imagine there were tears, there were smiles, there were hugs and undoubtedly there was prayer. Even as I write this, my heart swells to know two women, although cut from the same cloth and raised in the same household, were moving along two very different continuums—facing two very different breaking points. Despite these differences, one God—that same big, awesome God became real and personal that day. This God who perhaps at one time, was so big they too couldn't imagine His immense love and concern for them, would continue to be revealed in their lives for years to follow. As they traveled along their continuums together, a renewed bond and love for each other and the God they rediscovered would carry them through the most challenging of times—cancer, infidelity, heart failure, financial hardships and the loss of the only earthly father they knew.

When they departed, they would return to their separate lives. Both with journeys, a continuum of their own, but now the path and the purpose of those journeys was completely altered. In His wisdom God had set into motion a unique and explicit plan for the three women who were forever joined that day . . . she, she and me.

Chapter 3

Village and Friends

In the Nigerian Igbo culture, the proverb "Ora na azu nwa" has existed for centuries. It's meaning, *it takes the community (village) to raise a child*, is commonly attributed to being the source of a familiar American mantra, "It takes a village to raise a child." In 1996, the phrase was made popular by Hilary Clinton who adopted the proverb for the title of her book, *It takes a Village: And Other Lessons Children Teach Us.* As regarded by the Nigerian culture, it means the responsibility of cultivating children who are virtuous and morally sound lies not only with the parents, but also with the community or extended family.

While the concept spawned an era of enlightening discussions, academic and political debates, it fostered a genuine sense of discovery among those who encountered it. Did we believe it? Further, as Christians if we examine our own culture, can we compare it to our own scriptural truths? In my attempts to formulate my own perspective, a firm position by which I would raise my children, I spoke with Christians and non-Christians alike in search of a consensus. The opinions were varied and intriguing.

Many argued how Proverbs 13:24 clearly defines the roles of the parents— responsibilities that just couldn't be delegated. It reads, "Whoever spares the rod hates their children, but the one who loves their children is careful to discipline them." In Ephesians 6:4 the Apostle Paul admonishes the family head, "Fathers, do not provoke your children; instead bring them up in the training and instruction of the Lord." And in 1 Timothy 5:8, Paul again writes in very clear terms, "Anyone who does not provide for their relatives, and especially for their own household, has denied the faith and is worse than an unbeliever."

The argument: it is primarily the responsibility of the *head* of the household—which in most cases should be the father—to enforce discipline, set the tone and together with his parental partner (the mother), demonstrate a righteous and reputable lifestyle based in the teachings of Jesus Christ?

But what about the "non-conventional" family structure; where the father was either physically or emotionally absent and mother was left to ensure this biblical charge was carried out? As I tried to organize my thoughts, considering not only my plans as an existing parent, but also as a child raised by a single mother, I remembered those *other* verses; the countless teachings in which Christ emphasized the importance of community and the greatest of all commandments—to love one another.

I would examine Ecclesiastes 4: 9-12 which revealed,

> *Two are better than one, because they have a good reward for their toil. For if they fall, one will lift up his fellow. But woe to him who is alone when he falls and has not another to lift him up! Again, if two lie together, they keep warm, but how can one keep warm alone? And though a man might prevail against one who is alone, two will withstand him—a threefold cord is not quickly broken.*

I remembered Philippians 2:4 which cautioned,

> *Don't look out only for your own interests, but take an interest in others, too.*

I especially liked Romans 12:9-10 which said,

> *Don't just pretend to love others. Really love them. Hate what is wrong. Hold tightly to what is good. Love each other with genuine affection, and take delight in honoring each other.*

And when it came down to it, I recalled perhaps the Lord's most important direction for existing and thriving within a community, where in John 13:34-35 He said,

So now I am giving you a new commandment: Love each other.
Just as I have loved you, you should love each other. Your love for
one another will prove to the world that you are my disciples.

Perhaps those who believed the role of child-rearing lie solely within the hands of the parents would argue these verses could be applied to a myriad of conditions. My position? I would agree. The Bible truths that would outline God's expectations for love, community, friendship and forgiveness would be the same verses that would describe the ideal family structure—the network of people required to help that single mother move her child along the continuum. Indeed it takes a village, a Godly village of family and friends to raise a child.

Welcome to my village.

My village was comprised of an entire assortment of people. They were individuals from a variety of races, cultural backgrounds, economic statuses and family compositions. Some families were comprised of a single-parent dad or a grandmother raising everyone else's children while others consisted of families with a mom and a dad, two girls, two boys, a cat and a dog. My mother hated cats and dogs, but especially cats. Funny thing . . . I have two of each.

Within my village families lived separate lives with many common threads. For some it was the church at which we worshiped, the company at which people worked or the neighborhood in which we lived. Two fibers however, always remained the same . . . Merideth and God. They loved us both and would do anything, almost anything to ensure the two were inseparable.

Mother would come to know each of the village families at a particular point along her journey, our continuums. Time and circumstance was never the reason; God's appointment and purpose would continuously alter the village population and dynamics. Every so often a new family would move into the village, but they never left. Each one designated and orchestrated by God's greater plan. As mother and I moved along our continuums, the purpose of each family would slowly be revealed. The talents they possessed and the virtues they embodied were amazing and varied. Together they would facilitate remarkable miracles—miracles for Merideth.

Ruby. A beautiful stone, a symbol of impeccable taste and character—the ruby holds great meaning and significance. For me she was a remarkable soul possessing great strength and exuding even greater Godly wisdom. She always knew what to say and the exact moment in which to implant that tiny seed, a miracle in a message, to lift the troubled heart of a new mother. When mother first arrived to Kansas City, Ruby was one of the first families to join our village. It was 1976. Mother was a young black professional who just months before left Winnsboro, only in a daring effort to challenge her own strength and independence. Her burning love for Gran kept her close, her seven brothers and sisters doubted she could muster the courage required to leave the only angel she'd ever known.

Establishing roots in the big city meant growing pains, riding in carpools, renting from strangers and at one painful point along the journey, being robbed of every little bit she had. When home buying became the safest option, mother would search in Midtown. In an area comparable to the modern day Hampton Estates, she would ask her realtor, "Pardon me for asking, but would there happen to be any black families in this neighborhood?" The realtor replied, "Just look across the street . . ." and there sat busy working on the front porch, a very small boy—Ruby's son. Ruby and Betty would establish an eternal bond, one that would see them through countless joys, pains and unchartered waters. Their two continuums collided and their faiths were in the midst. The commonalities between the two would grow and thrive. They were sisters. She, the lone refuge when mother knew not one soul, and for Ruby, mother was the strength, the anchor when she needed her most. Ruby nurtured a house of men, two sons and a loving husband. When her husband, my Godfather died, Ruby cried. I had never seen her cry. My heart hurt deeply for her because she loved me so; she exuded an incessant love for everyone she encountered and never seemed to frown, yet I knew she was hurting. But mother was there, just as Ruby had been for her, mother was there.

Following Ruby would be John, Tony and Pearl. John was a single father of twin boys, boys he adopted at birth. He was an extraordinary man, the Frank Sinatra of fatherhood. He made being a father look good. At John's house, every meal was blessed and eaten from the dining room table and homework was done before six. It was though he glided on ice as he moved from the stove to the makeshift classroom he had fashioned for the twins and me whenever I would visit. He was the finest and fanciest of fathers. John welcomed me in his home often. When late-night meetings and business trips became the norm, mother made sure my home remained. No rule-bending and backtalk at John's. He was the father and I was captivated.

Tony was to Cliff as Pearl was to Claire—*Huxtable* of course. Tony and Pearl were my power couple; my black, strong, family-oriented power couple. Tied by a unity and love for family and for Christ, their achievements seemed limitless. These weren't just material, monetary gains, but children, lost souls, actual fruits they helped harvest for God's kingdom. Wow. "Who are these people?" I remembered thinking when I really began immersing myself into their culture regularly. Oh yes, they had a culture. Nothing about them was normal. Not the normal "black culture" I was used to. There was a mother, a father, two boys, a nice home, two steady jobs and love . . . a genuine love for everyone they met. They exchanged gifts every Christmas. Even I had a gift. After Easter Sunday service, the annual egg hunt would commence. I was invited, later my children were invited. Today, we're still invited. Who were these people?

Tony and Pearl would be mother's sounding board; her voices of reason, retreat and refuge when *our* world was too much to handle. They would listen, counsel, pray and advise, and frequently made visits. They were the Huxtables; most times I was ashamed to have them visit. Our house wasn't their house, but we were trying. Like watching an episode of *The Cosby Show,* we'd watch, steal some good tips and borrow from Tony and Pearl. This was a common practice in the village.

Going to Tony and Pearl's was a production—something you prepared for. I now know they never expected anyone to make a big deal, but we did. What they did, how they made you feel was indeed a big deal. I never wanted to go to Tony and Pearl's in plain sweats and a head scarf. Their family was together, presentable and nearly flawless so I wanted to get it together—or at least appear that way. When mother and I would fight, I'd say hurtful things or threaten to run away, I wondered if Tony and Pearl knew. I didn't want them to know, I wanted to be like them. I knew my poor choices would disappoint them greatly so I prayed they didn't know. In the village though, everyone knew. There was nothing secret about my behavior. Even still, Tony and Pearl never changed. They never let me know they knew. Their house was still my house and with every visit, I dressed up for Tony and Pearl.

Then there was Christine. Christine was a survivor. Although I didn't know it until much later, she had lived life. Every earthly pain known to man—she encountered; she knew them well. Domestic violence, untimely repeated deaths of friends and siblings, a failed marriage, caring for children no one wanted, running for her life . . . she knew each tale all too well. It seemed as though Christine had all the answers—both in life and the Bible. Mother met Christine when she first joined what would be our church home. Christine taught the adult Bible class on Sunday's where she brought dynamic and personal application to each lesson. Christine knew hurt, but she also knew God. She spoke openly about both, setting the stage for what was real and what was possible. She was much like Moses, who after being in the presence of God, descended from Mount Sinai unknowingly his face aglow with the awesome glory of the Lord; a radiance that would remain with him until his death (Exodus 34:29).

Christine demonstrated a radiance and a trust in God I had never seen. Others described it, testified about it and mother lived it. But Christine, she had bathed in it. Satan was using life and all its devices to destroy her (John 10:10); he knew she was a solider, an asset to Christ's heavenly kingdom and a threat to Evil's earthly pit. Her life exuded a humility and faithfulness like that of Job, a man who lost his family, his home and his wealth as part of a test of his faith. When burdens seemed unbearable, temptation and selfish pity would echo through the words of Job's wife, "Are you still holding on to your integrity? Curse God and die! (Job 2:9)" But like Job, Christine would stand. In spite of every grief, every loss, she held fast to her faith and God's unfailing hand.

And who could forget the Mackays? If Tony and Pearl were the Huxtables, the Mackays were the Bradys; the Jesus-fearing, confidence-building, sports-loving, milk-drinking Bradys. *(I caution you not to be offended by my blunt use of the words "white" and "black." You'll soon see why the raw nomenclature is so important)*

Now picture this. I first came to know the Mackays through their children who would be my classmates at two private Christian schools—my mother's last resort to salvage the future I was destroying daily. I had come from a culture where white people were present, but not personal. I knew *of* some white families, was fairly friendly with those I knew and played with at school, but that was the extent of it. As a child, all of us—black, white, girls, and boys—

were modern day bullies and didn't realize it. The hurtful stereotypes we held and the discouraging words we uttered against each other were common then. It's hard to believe these same words are causing the suicides, hate crimes and intolerant behaviors of so many children today.

In my culture, white people had lice, kissed their dogs in the mouth and washed their hair every day. To them, I was lazy, disruptive in class, ghetto in my conversation and always needed help with my math homework. Were these stereotypes or truths unspoken? Over time my truth was validated to be mere myths. The Mackays were not the stereotypical white family. They revealed a culture completely foreign to me and dispelled every "truth" I had amassed about *those* people. The Mackays would teach me invaluable lessons—how being on time is a reflection of good character and commitment, why trustworthy people must work hard and do honorable things, and how even the fallen are forgiven. Not only are they forgiven, but they are cherished and fostered back to good health. This was Christ's family. Every day at the Mackays wasn't always roses and sunshine. They experienced pain, disappointment and days of unpredictability; but they were a family who lived and thrived by the teachings of Jesus Christ.

Like John and the boys, every meal at the Mackays was family occasion, a Thanksgiving dinner in itself. Food was prepared well in advance—an array of choices from *all five* food groups. Meal settings for each member were complete with fork, knife, spoon, napkins and plates; and of course there was milk. It's funny how I remember this small but very significant gesture. Mama and Papa Mackay nurtured their children with love, discipline, sound Godly advice and the physical substance required to be successful. This substance was milk. Milk would grace the table at every meal—five-course to single snack—the Mackays embodied the liquid as *the* choice for champions.

Early on, I scoffed at this mockery of fairytale living; secretly despising the fact this was not a ritual in my own home. Yeah, mother had offered me milk a time or two. But most times it was reserved for cereal, nothing more. I realize now it wasn't so much the milk I longed for, but the relationship, the communion and the hope the beverage represented. The Mackays were who I wanted to be. They were where I longed to dwell forever and ever. In my village I had so many families, so many options for love, for fellowship and friends. But my village had the Mackays . . . and they had milk.

As our village grew, the number of families did as well. In time came the Austins, the Kings, the Davis' and of course Sister Gilbert—I *loved* Sister Gilbert. My village would become a culture in its own right; a movement of people traveling along the continuums of life and Christian character. We were joined by so many pieces, possibilities, heartaches and opportunities. Above all, we were working together—a body of many parts in clean synchronization—moving toward the common goal of glorifying God with our lives.

I love 1 Corinthians 12 for so many reasons, mostly for its description of the body. In my case, the blueprint demonstrating the handiwork and cleaver orchestration in which God had constructed my village. It reveals how each of us represents a very significant but specific part of the larger Christian body; making us an absolutely vital part of God's work as a whole. It reads,

> *[1]Now about the gifts of the Spirit, brothers and sisters, I do not want you to be uninformed . . .*
>
> *[4] There are different kinds of gifts, but the same Spirit distributes them. [5] There are different kinds of service, but the same Lord. [6] There are different kinds of working, but in all of them and in everyone it is the same God at work.*
>
> *[7] Now to each one the manifestation of the Spirit is given for the common good. [8] To one there is given through the Spirit a message of wisdom, to another a message of knowledge by means of the same Spirit, [9] to another faith by the same Spirit, to another gifts of healing by that one Spirit, [10] to another miraculous powers, to another prophecy, to another distinguishing between spirits, to another speaking in different kinds of tongues, and to still another the interpretation of tongues. [11] All these are the work of one and the same Spirit, and he distributes them to each one, just as he determines.*
>
> *[12] Just as a body, though one, has many parts, but all its many parts form one body, so it is with Christ. [13] For we were all baptized by one Spirit so as to form one body—whether Jews or Gentiles, slave or free—and we were all given the one Spirit to drink. [14] Even so the body is not made up of one part but of many.*

15 Now if the foot should say, "Because I am not a hand, I do not belong to the body," it would not for that reason stop being part of the body. 16 And if the ear should say, "Because I am not an eye, I do not belong to the body," it would not for that reason stop being part of the body. 17 If the whole body were an eye, where would the sense of hearing be? If the whole body were an ear, where would the sense of smell be? 18 But in fact God has placed the parts in the body, every one of them, just as he wanted them to be. 19 If they were all one part, where would the body be? 20 As it is, there are many parts, but one body.

21 The eye cannot say to the hand, "I don't need you!" And the head cannot say to the feet, "I don't need you!" 22 On the contrary, those parts of the body that seem to be weaker are indispensable, 23 and the parts that we think are less honorable we treat with special honor. And the parts that are unpresentable are treated with special modesty, 24 while our presentable parts need no special treatment. But God has put the body together, giving greater honor to the parts that lacked it, 25 so that there should be no division in the body, but that its parts should have equal concern for each other. 26 If one part suffers, every part suffers with it; if one part is honored, every part rejoices with it.

27 Now you are the body of Christ, and each one of you is a part of it. 28 And God has placed in the church first of all apostles, second prophets, third teachers, then miracles, then gifts of healing, of helping, of guidance, and of different kinds of tongues. 29 Are all apostles? Are all prophets? Are all teachers? Do all work miracles? 30 Do all have gifts of healing? Do all speak in tongues? Do all interpret? 31 Now eagerly desire the greater gifts. And yet I will show you the most excellent way.

As a body, each family within my village would carry its own integral and unique gift—a gift transformed into responsibility, a responsibility to build, carry and care for each member, including me. Verse twenty-six foretold the continuum would be unpredictable, oftentimes painful. But the charge would remain—to suffer, celebrate and survive as a village. Sure enough, trials did follow as perilous times persisted; but the village, the concert of strangers who morphed into lifelong friends, would stand.

It would be Ruby who would make that short jaunt across the street when I threatened to run away and never return. She talked me off the ledge so many times, with her tender face she'd smile and say, "I love you, I truly, truly love you," it was then I knew my threats had hurt her so.

It was John who would attend my graduation ceremony; the completion of my Master's degree nearly ten years, four kids, and one shaky marriage later. Life was getting better and that day would signify so many things. It was John who was there, radiating with honor at the sight of his village daughter. No doubt his mind danced back to distant memories of me, him and the boys working from the extravagant dining room table he so generously fashioned into our classroom workspace. He had contributed to this moment and to the woman that stood before him. He was there to celebrate *our* victory.

Tony and Pearl would be at the graduations as well—high school and college, and at the birthday celebrations of every new child. It didn't matter how they came to be or how many more were to follow. Every Christmas each child received a gift, every Easter a basket of goodies and delights would await. When mother and I were in the midst of great turbulence and strife, they ensured laughter, good times, and life itself would carry on. They would be our normal.

Christine would be the counselor, my mother's Carey (Papa) to keep us all upright. When wits were frayed and prayers seemed practically impossible, Christine emerged on cue. Her door was always open, a shelter and a place to refuel. There was good food, but great structure. Time and experience had taught her well and when tough love was required, Christine carried the torch. Later at my most fragile of times, Christine would carry me—my tears, my panic, my insurmountable sense of fright. She was wise and on time. She was my voice of reason; a distant but unmistakable light.

The Mackays were my hope. Hopes of what was, what could be, and what God willed for our lives. They knew what was possible with a little love and a lift. They were the safety net catching us when we tried and picking us up when we fell short. It would be the Mackays who would give me my first job, demonstrating values of hard work, accountability and honesty. They were my family in a box—a treasure from God himself; one far more precious than a lifetime's riches could ever amount to be. I was sixteen when I conceived and just seventeen when I became a mother. It would be the Mackays who carried me from menace to mommy. Without a single word of judgment or even uttering a hint of disgust, they would materialize their love as a tiny gift box on my doorstep. They showed up, they stayed, fed babies, changed diapers, sang lullabies and prayed. They never left. Thirteen years they remained and they never ever left.

Supported by our village families, mother did all she could to care for the new bundle that was now hers. She built a home, established a foundation with rules, a sense of order, bedtime stories and TV dinners. Ok, so she didn't learn to cook as a child, but she adopted values that were vital to her survival in a grown-up world. She learned the importance of education, working hard to provide for yourself and your family, and that personal sacrifice is often required when caring for those solely reliant on you. Mother said "no" a lot. Out of concern and sometimes prevention, risks were not things she willingly liked to take. Like any child, I despised the word "no," I could care less about risks and I didn't understand why I couldn't have my way. And like all children, I progressed through my terrible twos, threes and perhaps even fours. But progression never became growth. I was troubled in every aspect of the word.

In elementary school I was bullied, left out of playground games, called "nappyhead" and even smacked in the face. I hated going to school. The girls were mean—I didn't fit in with any of the cool cliques—and the boys thought my clothes were old; it was hardly a place of wonderment and joy. Unfortunately the only memories I have of the 3rd and 4th grade are of moments spent outside the classroom—well, except for that one time when I was sent to the timeout corner in the back of the classroom. It was an oriental folding partition fashioned to serve as a barrier separating me from the rest of the class. I'm not sure why I was sent to the corner—for something ridiculously egregious I'm sure. Well, the teacher somehow forgot I was back there and left me in the corner the entire day. It wasn't until the kids had gone and the lights were turned out and I whimpered a, "Miss Thompson, can I come out now," she realized I had been forgotten.

Not to say my behavior was undeserving of reprimand, I was disruptive, inattentive and yearned for attention. I was always talking, getting out of my seat, I even stole show-and-tell toys from other children because my toys at home where nothing like theirs. And for whatever reason, I wanted more than their toys. I wanted their lives, their moms and dads, their sisters and brothers; I wanted my world to be as blissful as theirs appeared.

The other kids didn't understand how I could have a mom and not a dad. They poked fun of me as children playfully do, unaware of how devastating the thought of being abnormal was. I was impressionable and reactive so I quickly countered with the strategy I knew best; I denied who I really was and imaginatively concocted a world of my own. Soon my lies became the only existence I knew.

One morning as I dressed for school as part of my normal routine, I must have had a horrible nightmare or felt dreadfully seditious when I awoke, because I set a plan in motion to be someone else—a girl who had just lived through the unthinkable. Crying profusely, face swollen and hair a mess, I walked into Ms. Thompson's classroom and said, "I want to kill myself, my father just died." I went on to explain how he had been shot right before my eyes the night before. With as much vivid and gruesome detail my cunning mind could muster I described how he bled and suffered; I had nothing else to live for.

Well of course Ms. Thompson called mother right away, only to discover the story was a horrendous tale of deceit. Mother simply could not fathom what had caused me to devise such a terrible tragedy. She became consumed with trying to understand just what had gotten into me, what went wrong, and if help was even possible.

Visits to pediatricians, psychologists and psychiatrists became the norm. Family counselors, Christian and otherwise, couldn't quite understand just why I had strayed so far. "Has she been through any recent trauma . . . lost a loved one, survived a divorce" they would probe. Mother would mention the adoption and then reject the notion quickly that such a tremendous act of love had gone horribly wrong.

When practitioners diagnosed me with Attention Deficit Disorder and insisted my problems could only be treated by medical interventions, mother adamantly contended, "I refuse to accept that . . . you're not putting my baby on any medications." That would be the last time she took me to a shrink, and in faith she pressed on in her pursuit for answers, trusting God's will would still be done.

The more she tried to intervene, the more I rebelled. I didn't want this life, I didn't want this existence. I longed to live the life of someone else. Whose life was irrelevant compared to the why. I was searching, desperate for a connection and a sense of pride about whom and whose I was. Despite mother's attempt to reassure me I was hers, I wanted more, something greater; I needed a purpose that I could call my own—one that made perfect sense.

> *For we are God's workmanship, created in Christ Jesus to do good works, which God prepared in advance for us to do. (Ephesians 2:10)*

Mother was dedicated to me, my aspirations *and* my deviations. As a single mother she endured the many cycles of adolescence and young adult development as all parents do. As a parent of one, her weights were intensified, so were her joys. Mother was always proud of me; even when I failed to perform and model my behaviors after the standards she knew God had established and predestined for me. In 2011, she shared a story with a local news publication *Jackie Magazine*, in which she described her admiration for the overzealous and determined child God had endowed her with. An excerpt from the article reads:

> *Betty Neal was taking an early walk that morning.*
>
> *It had become a routine, a quiet moment in which she could pause and think and view the picture of her life up to that point. She and her daughter, Merideth, were living in a home off Blue Ridge Boulevard in Kansas City. It was the mid-1980s and, like most mothers, Neal had a lot on her mind.*
>
> *Returning home, Neal was surprised to find Merideth, then 6 years old, outside, holding onto the railing.*

"Merideth liked to sleep," her mother said. "So I was surprised to see her outside. I asked her what was wrong, and she looked at me and said she'd thought I'd left her."

Assuring her daughter that she had not, that she would never leave her, Merideth turned around and went back inside.

"I asked her where she was going and she said she was going to call the police back and tell them her mother was home."

The story, which brings out laughter in Betty each time she tells it, seems simple, but it's not. Like many children, Merideth had unknowingly shown her mother, through words and actions, the future.

"It showed me that she could work things out," she said. "I could see she was a good thinker." (Excerpt from *Merideth Parrish: From bad choices to good, a life in transition. by Jeff Martin*)

Today, when we recall this story together along with countless others—we laugh; for some stories we cry. At one time we cried tears of pain and distress, tears for unspoken strife and broken spirits. Now, we share misty eyes and smiles of jubilation, celebrating the reuniting of family, an eternal friendship and our shared Christian faith. In harmonious reflection we echo the words of a familiar gospel hymn . . . *if it had not been for the Lord on my side, where would I be, where would I be?*

Chapter 4
A Season of Pain, Pressure and Purpose

The episodes of pain and tested patience were prolific. Days and nights of frustration would turn into weeks of praying, fasting and consulting with friends. As mother continued her fervent search for answers, I continued to spiral out of control. It would be her close personal friends like Tony and Pearl, her surrogate sisters Christine, Ruby, Aldoria and Joyce and her birth sisters Barbara and Evelyn who would be her voices of reassurance and shoulders of support when motherhood seemed unbearable.

As I reflect on those times, feelings of guilt and disbelief always seem to surface. I remember some things vaguely; others have left vivid impressions—wounds that only Christ can heal. I was probably ten or eleven when pain reached its peak. Performing poorly in school and threatening to flee from home at every possible opportunity, church became my only real safe haven. Although attendance averaged about twenty-five members on any given Sunday, my intimate church family nested within a large, cathedral-style building as was a place of refuge, even for a dysfunctional child. At church I had friends, people liked me. I couldn't tell if it was because they had to or because they simply felt sorry for me. Here, I wasn't an outsider like I was at my public elementary school. I was accepted, just me—my troublesome tantrums, untamable talking and my voice; my love of song and singing God's praises became my voice.

At church, worship was wonderful—it was electrifying, but the rules were strict. There was a time for praising, a time for singing and dancing, and a time for solitude and prayer. Then there was the sermon. For us kids, there was no talking during the sermon. Only the adults belted a lively, "Amen!" or "Praise the Lord!" or even "Preach, preacher," but not the children. It almost felt as though it were forbidden. I always wanted to shout like I had seen some of the older saints do—even raise my hands and close my eyes when we would sing,

Oh, I want to see Him look upon his face . . . But I was worried. I was unsure of how I would appear to my friends. These were the *only* true friends I had, so I had to play it safe. I couldn't appear too churchy; that just wasn't cool.

What was cool was singing in the choir; especially with the older kids—the teens. I was an adolescent, but not quite a teenager. To me the teens *were* church. I watched them, marveled at them and wanted so much to be around and be like them. As the teens grew older so did I. With at least a three-year gap between me and the youngest teen though, I tried so much to remain part of the in-group, but my popularity and likeability was waning fast. It was happening again, I was slowly being rejected.

Like most church youth groups we participated in outings, held gatherings like Vacation Bible School at the church, and rehearsed for Christmas musicals and Easter productions. I loved rehearsals, mainly for the singing. I loved to sing. As my voice developed some of the teens started taking notice. Choir directors picked me to lead solos, the girls with the "good voices" asked me to stand next to them during rehearsals, and the boys were complimenting my voice. I imagine I sounded no better than a shaky newborn bird, but it didn't matter because they all noticed. It was a feeling and a sense of belonging I couldn't escape. I was back in the in-crowd. My relationships, like my newfound voice was flourishing. Invitations to girls-only sleepovers, birthday parties and weekend hangouts were a regular. This is what it felt like to belong.

Every so often I worried, "what if I lose this feeling, what if they find out what I'm really like—at home, with my mother?" If they discovered how careless I was, noncompliant of rules and authority, a real misbehaved child—would they still like me? Would they want me in their company? Prayer requests must have turned into church-chatter in the foyer—because worst fears soon became reality. Cliques were forming and I was not on the roster. There were the occasional close friends who liked me in spite of my reputation but it simply wasn't enough. I wanted more—more friends, more of the attention. I wanted the teens to want me around. Needless to say, my childhood life was a rollercoaster of being "in" and being "out."

At ten years old, I was fearless. Potato sack race at the church picnic, sign me up. Basketball with the boys on Youth Night Fridays, bring it on. I clamored for family, for camaraderie and for personal connections however I could get them. In my crusade to become all things popular, I failed to establish and to understand boundaries. When you're ten, most of this happens for you. Your parents lay ground rules clearly outlining what will and will not be tolerated and how poor choices are often accompanied by negative consequences. My mother had laid these ground rules several times, but I simply refused to listen and adhere. A single instance though, a shameful act within the walls of my safe haven, would soon test these nonexistent boundaries; it would be a moment that would change me forever—my limits, my value of self and my pursuit of everything that was pure.

He was older, much older than me in fact. A member of our church, a musician, a scholar, an athlete—he was one of the "it kids"—*he*, was going places. I never really thought much about him simply because his very stature was daunting; it was adult-like and based on my intolerance of adults and authority, I thought of him as just *another one of them*. I was friends with his friends—girls and boys alike—we shared the same inner circle. On Sundays, Wednesdays and the occasional Friday, we shared much more. There was the common place and principles of worship—from the piano he played, from the choir stand I sang. A professed faith in God—He prayed, I prayed. In Sunday school class he teased me for mispronouncing freshman level adjectives and I called him a name—usually the most foolish and awkward thing I could think of (bear in mind I was only ten).

What we didn't share was an understanding of why. Why *were* there regular encounters between him and me? Why would he wait and linger in corners, empty bathrooms and dark hallways to meet me, oftentimes unknowingly frightening me? Why was I asked to do things, touch places, take positions and say things to a teenage boy, exuding sexual behaviors ten year old girls are never taught? My response to which was to pretend I knew exactly what my role was, for fear of what would happen if I didn't. I was touched, caressed and kissed in ways I didn't understand. And why didn't it stop—after the first, second and even third time? During hide-and-go seek games and church-sponsored overnight stays—why didn't it stop? There would be conversations, explicit conversations. He would say what we wanted, how he wanted it and would correct my juvenile missteps along the way. When directed I would attempt to comply—hiding my humiliation and fear behind a giggle, and a nervous,

"I can't do that . . ." I hated the way he touched me and the way his clothing smelled. It was an odor that lay deeply seeded in a painful memory, one that still lingers on.

And where was God in all this? Did He know what was going on, did He care? I waited for Him. Every Sunday I prayed for my heavenly Father to intervene. In my heart I just couldn't feel Him, I was convinced He was watching, yet He had turned his back on me, little ol' sinful me.

As the encounters continued, they grew. Boy must have spoken to boy, because the next one came. By this time I was eleven or twelve. I had grown uncomfortable, distrusting and downright angry. I told mother, church friend, whoever would listen. But unfortunately my history of lies, defiance and deception preceded me. People listened but nothing changed. Over time the first boy lost interest, moving on to activities and people more appropriate for his age. Conventional dating soon ensued and girlfriend after girlfriend would be his special guest at Sunday's service. I often caught myself wondering, "Does she know about us, about me?" At one point, I thought I even felt a twinge of jealously but realize now, I was tainted and confused. Would this confusion between what was wrong and what I believed to be love completely misguide my relationship bearings in the future? It would and it did.

When I had had enough, I learned to refuse boy #2. Was it because I was an eleven year old now feeling rejected by her first pursuer, or had I really had enough? The latter was true. I was tired of running. Trips to the bathroom during morning worship service were now far and in between for fear of what lurked in the parsonage shadows. Innocence was gone.

The episodes of sexual molestation were a very small portion of my larger church fabric. The majority of my memories consist of unforgettable worship experiences, weeknight choir rehearsals, preparing for the yearly National Convention Bible Quiz and moments with Sister Gilbert. In the black church, it is a common practice to address one another in a very domestic and intimate nature—prefacing any reference to the formal name with "sister" or "brother."

I loved Sister Gilbert. A bubbly woman with a witty sense of humor and unceasing love for God, Sister Gilbert was enthralled with living for God. She loved the Word—teaching it, studying it, applying it to life's situations.

Together, she and mother were the Bible ambassadors of the church. Sister Gilbert taught the children's Sunday school classes and my mother, the adult's. I often look back and marvel at their ministerial positions—the backbone of the small, but significant church family. When others were leaving, starting families and moving on, the two Bible ambassadors remained.

Unsurprisingly, Sister Gilbert loved children; not just her own, but all children—those she knew, those she just met, those without a safe and stable home. I was no exception. Sister Gilbert was like the family doctor of my childhood village, she was a master of her trade. Her specialty: helping children find balance between their needs, their feelings and their desires. Professionally she was a social worker turned school counselor so she understood and embraced the importance of fostering opportunities. She understood that while socioeconomic disparities, poor education and an unstable home environment created certain constraints in which children couldn't always get what they wanted, there are certain visions and dreams they must be encouraged to achieve. She was our fairy godmother. In her world and the faith in which she walked, nothing was impossible with God *(Luke 1:37)*.

Called to be a nurturer of children at an early age, she spent most of her life caring for the children of others—siblings' children, her children's children and even her grandchildren's children. Among these she cared for was her granddaughter, Jae. Jae was nearly three years older than me, but embraced me just the same. She was my big sister. Growing up together in our little church of less than fifty, we were inseparable. It was with Jae I shared my most private thoughts, inner secrets and cherished moments. She was there when the boys stole my innocence. She believed me, she protected me when she could . . . she cared. When others learned of my rowdy behavior and mouthy demeanor, they scattered. Not Jae. Jae remained close by—showing me the ropes, giving me guidance from a teen's perspective—explaining how to "chill out" and "just be cool."

I connected with Jae like no one else before her. Our friendship wasn't threatening, it wasn't scripted, it was real. Now, when I try to understand what exactly it was about our relationship that was so infatuating, I realize it wasn't infatuation at all. It was a connection of commonality. Jae too was the product of a nonconventional upbringing being raised by her grandmother, and was a willful challenger of adult authority. Her depravities were certainly not as bold and disconcerting as mine, but her adolescent complexities were intriguing . . . and in some respects, encouraging. I felt a sense of comfort with our mutual desire to be cared for and cared about.

When together with Jae and Sister Gilbert, I was in a good place. Mother and Sister Gilbert were like sisters—even before there was Merideth and Jae. There would be trips together, both church-related and not; family dinners, weekend hangouts, gospel concerts and caroling at senior centers. As a child who oftentimes interpreted joy as superficial and momentary thrills, times with Sister Gilbert and Jae were just plain fun; carefree, unfiltered fun. Little did I realize, these moments—these visits to aid and engage with others—would be the cornerstones that would later create my desire to minister and to serve. Sister Gilbert knew and mother would pray; these moments would help produce the authenticity and materialization of a much greater purpose—my Christian character.

> *For he chose us in him before the creation of the world to be holy and blameless in his sight. In love he predestined us to be adopted as his sons through Jesus Christ, in accordance with his pleasure and will. (Ephesians 1:4-5)*

Chapter 5

Coming to Calvary

By the time I was twelve, the realization I would soon drown in the overcrowded classrooms and alienation of underpaid teachers in public school, hit my mother like a ton of bricks. With school counselors throwing up their hands in despair and medical practitioners eager to diagnose me with a myriad of behavioral disorders, mother prayed incessantly for God's intervention. She would tell me, "I prayed and fasted for my daughter, daily—I prayed and I prayed." Even today her eyes swell with tears as she tries to hide the once paralyzing fear that her daughter was destined for destruction. "I would just cry out to the Lord, tell me what to do God, tell me . . ."

It was in these times her village, her network of friends grew strong and unified in purpose—determined to accomplish spiritual victory in the life of one very vulnerable child. Together they would join, pray, speak weekly, even daily to find solutions. In time, God would move as He had so many times before— offering the first of many solutions to come.

Calvary Lutheran was a midsized private school offering elementary and middle school education rooted in Christian principles, discipline and discipleship. Because of its location in the central part of Kansas City it was comprised of a unique blend of students and families—black and white, various languages, financial statuses and household demographics. There I would travel through grades five through eight with countless exposure to people like me—kids with problems, one mom, no dad; some, just getting by. Over the course of four years I made friends, real friends . . . . friends like Jae.

These friends were different. They were warm, welcoming and surprisingly genuine. Needless to say, school was still school. Cliques and clubs ruled the playground. There were the girls who wore boys' clothes. There were boys who were good in science, math and athletics. There were girls who chased after the boys and there were the kids whose moms and dads worked long hours; this was my club. We were the first ones to arrive in the morning, and the last ones to leave at night. I didn't mind being associated with this group as they became known as the who's who of Calvary. Most nights we made the short trip across the street to the public library. We were diligent about our studies and took advantage of the after-school time to get a head start on homework. But perhaps more so than homework, we were serious about our skills, yes, this group had flair. We were an inventive group. Time to kill meant time to relate to each other, it meant bonding through our favorite pastimes, our annoying pitfalls, even a platonic crush or two. Within the group we had singers, dancers, wrappers and artists. This was my village, my very own community of friends.

Calvary became the best of both worlds. I found people like me who loved what I loved. Having discovered a burning desire for worship at my own church I was mesmerized by the joy and freedom of singing God's praises. Calvary was the platform for my voice to soar. I joined a girls group whose sole focus was to bring hip hop to our weekly and very Lutheran chapel services. I auditioned for lead roles in springtime musicals like *Fat, Fat Jehoshaphat* and performed in my first talent show. (I must have been going through a very "hip-hop" phase as our 4-member group of very sassy, black 7th and 8th graders pranced all over the stage to Johnny Gill's *Rub you the Right Way*) Need I say more?

The school would give me a foundation, a broader knowledge base revealing who I was both in life and in Christ. It would be the catalyst for becoming the person God destined me to become.

When I think of the institution I knew as Calvary and the biblical reference to Calvary's cross, I compare myself—even as a middle-schooler—to the two criminals who hung next to Jesus the night He was crucified *(Luke 23:33-43)*. Unlike Jesus, both men were guilty, actual offenders previously convicted of crimes with offenses punishable by death. As they hung there in the presence of Christ, both men had the opportunity to confess their sins, turn from their aggressions if even for just a moment, before they took their final breathes embarking to the places in which they would spend eternity.

One of the men would reject Jesus, hurling insults and questioning His very deity. Selfishly he would challenge Jesus and His power to save the criminal and Jesus himself. The other however, would recognize in that moment, exactly who Jesus was. The "ah-hah" miracle had occurred. A life of sin, corruption and criminal behavior would be forever forgiven and erased. The criminal acknowledged the saving power of Jesus Christ, asking Jesus to take him unto himself—a final resting place with the Lord in heaven. I like to think the first criminal was at a very premature point along his continuum. At Calvary's cross and what would be his final hope for redemption, he faced an opportunity to make an eternal and literally, life-altering decision. But he rejected God, thus sealing his fate.

At Calvary Lutheran—my Calvary's cross, I was the first criminal. Granted I had not committed any unspeakable offenses, but I was lost; still wandering, still lying, still cheating and still in need of a Savior. It didn't matter I was fully immersed in the presence of God. Just like that criminal, God himself was in my midst. In my four years at Calvary I attended well over 300 hours of chapel service, memorized more than 200 Bible verses and even recited the confessions of faith from the Small Catechism as written by Martin Lutheran (impressive huh?); to God, not so much. If I had died as an eighth-grader, none of my scholarly cohabitation with Christ would have mattered. He dwelled well around me, nowhere inside me.

Some of my best days were spent at Calvary. What about friends? I had lots of them here. Many of which I still see and chat with from time to time. Calvary was also the birthplace of my first boyfriend (pardon the cliché). His name was Tim. One would think the pursuit of a boyfriend for an obviously unstable girl with emotional baggage and trust issues would be a recipe for disaster . . . but Tim didn't know that. You would also think in a Lutheran school, where the predominant race of students were white with straight flowing hair—the kind that slicks back after a field trip to the pool in July—that me, kinky haired, black-skinned me wouldn't possibly be chosen by a white boy named Tim. But I was. I was chosen by Tim.

Tim's approach was something out of a *Junie B. Jones* story. I remember it well. It was English class, right before recess. We were just weeks away from our eighth grade dance, my first formal attempt to look, smell and behave as a young girl ought. As I was falling into my rhythm—finding myself, discovering my voice and getting to be quite the basketball player—I was learning to mellow. Needless to say, all was not perfect in my world of adolescent behavior, but I was discovering the "me" underneath. I had my dress, my mother's blessing to go (I had worked ridiculously hard to stay in line and out of trouble), but no date. Deep inside and as she expressed verbally a few times, mother thought the idea of an eighth grade dance was nonsense, "utter foolishness." But I wanted to go and every other foolish eighth grader had a date.

I liked Tim, but never really in "that way." He was easy on the eyes, boasted an uneventful bowl-shaped haircut and was very polite; almost too polite. He was soft-spoken but loved a good rowdy game of kickball. At recess, I always made a point to be on Tim's team. He would joke with me and I would toss the ball at his head. This meant he would get hurt and I'd be ejected from the game. I figured we'd be banished to the sidelines, forced to become spectators for different reasons. Either way, I would get my time with Tim. I wanted him to know I liked him and was curious, would he dare like me—a black girl, with kinky dark hair?

Time after time I would set my clever kickball plan into motion, but never had the guts to capitalize on our sideline time. He would sit glaring at me, too embarrassed and unwilling to return to the game. I was racking up disciplinary actions from every foul play so I had to act quickly or my hard-earned outing to the dance would be nothing but a distant memory never to be experienced.

Finally, a week before the dance I built up enough gumption to ask him. I was going to do it. I had rehearsed my lines at nausea. That day I would be nice to Tim. I wouldn't plunge the thick red rubber ball at his head—the consequences were too risky. I would volunteer to be first pitcher up. I would make sure we were on opposing teams and the pitch to Tim would be easy. Truth is, I have no idea how the game ended, but I remember "the ask." After recess, as we were going in I would offer a simple, "Hey Tim, my mom is taking me to the dance on Saturday. I was wondering if you wanted to ride with me." Instead, something very different and unexpected emerged. Apparently I was so nervous I asked Tim to be my boyfriend. Call it a Freudian slip or the faux pas of a frisky eighth grader, but by the end of the day, Tim and I were dating. He said yes. Other girls had asked, but Tim had chosen me.

The dance and the following weeks were all a blur. I was on cloud nine (ten and eleven) and then reality set in. I had experienced my first true crush but realized Tim was too nice and frankly, I was too unstable. I broke up with Tim for reasons I can't begin to imagine, but will never forget my first date, my first dance and my first kiss with tiny, timid Tim.

While thoughts of Calvary Lutheran give way to great joy, a small but painful memory remains. It is a gentle reminder of the friendships found at my school and Calvary's cross, a reminder of friends made and friends lost. As my eighth grade year was coming to a close I lost a very good friend. It wasn't natural, it wasn't by accident; it was her choice.

Ryan was beautiful. I often found myself gazing at her during silent reading time in Mrs. Rivers' class. Her flawless skin was milky white only further accented by the honey blond spiked hair that dressed her petite face. I had never seen hair like Ryan's. Sometimes her hair was black, red, and on occasion a deep orange. Ryan exposed all of us to a different type of life. She lived out loud and loved God hard. She was a firecracker when she couldn't get her way and she was friends with people we never thought existed—well at least I didn't.

It was because of Ryan I discovered what it meant to be gay. Ryan knew gay people and was friends with them; genuinely befriended them. Her relationships, even her public conversations reinforced how Christians, despite the conflict in lifestyle and beliefs we share with all types of people, still have a spiritual obligation to love and embrace *those* people. Each day our class would end with prayer. We would call off the names of loved ones, friends and pets who required God's attention. And every day, the names of Ryan's special friends—two in particular would remain. They were living with AIDS and Ryan prayed, not for their salvation, but that God's peace and presence would surround them. Every day those names were read, even when no one else had a need or name to offer. And every day those names remained until the day those two friends died. I miss Ryan and think about her almost every day.

For me, Ryan's life—her story reaffirmed I wasn't the only one living with shadows and pains so hurtful the thought of bearing them much longer was more than what sometimes one child can stand. Why was she hurting so? Why didn't she tell me—I was her friend? For a while I didn't understand. I even challenged my own sense of courage. Did I have what it takes to end my life? Was my pain, my past and my unworthiness of the Savior so great that I would take His place, make an empty attempt to die for my own sins? I quickly rejected the notion only for it to resurface years later when conditions did get worse, when the bruises became visible and there were no more shadows in which to hide.

> *Then Jesus said, "Come to me, all of you who are weary and carry heavy burdens, and I will give you rest. (Matthew 11:28)*

Chapter 6
Lutheran, Black or Bastard?

Most people would agree, particularly parents, high school is one of the most critical times in a child's life. While it's a period plagued with broken hearts, bad hair days, acne breakouts and biweekly breakups, it's a time when human character is defined—at least initially. It is an era in which young leaders, followers, professionals and dreamers emerge; each with their own individuality and determination to leave their mark somehow, somewhere. It is in high school where the formation of groups, cliques, allies and enemies really solidify. Young boys transition into men and young girls either pledge a life of purity or pursue the loss of innocence. Some parents are more prepared than others and the journey through *Life Senior High* represents a period of validation—gratifying proof that all the nights of praying, bedtime stories and painful punishments were not done in vein.

For parents like my mother, careful planning and preparation was simply not enough. God's will would reveal a time of testing, tenderness and tough decisions. His plan for our family required a much more challenging journey, one designed to strengthen our character and ultimately draw us closer to Him.

Mother's preparations for my voyage into high school were nothing short of extensive planning and fervent prayers. Would I go back to public school or be bussed to the nearest all-girls institution for prim and proper training . . . do those even exist anymore? I had such a difficult time trying to find my rhythm, my niche and really any good common sense in public schools, would a private establishment make a difference?

It appeared the Christian culture was indeed having an impact. Calvary had been a good move. I wasn't totally cured, but I was finding my way, my voice and what would be my life's purpose. My teachers didn't take any mess and certainly weren't intimated by my insatiable sense of lying and insubordination. They tackled my temper and my attitude with the sharpest sword—the Word of God.

After many consultations with me, immediate family and the members of our village, mother would decide to send me to Calvary's sequel if you will, Lutheran High School or LHS. Eighth grade at Calvary was such an interesting time because its conclusion was a mini passage in its own right. In December, just six months before our last moments at Calvary, hallways and lunchrooms were all abuzz with talk of "Where are you going to high school?" We would talk as though we were being drafted by a major league sports team. There were countless options, plenty of schools to choose from—both public and private.

Because Calvary was a Christian school, the kids who were continuing on in their course for spiritual enlightenment (through a Christian education) were considered the lucky ones; I'm sure some kids didn't think of themselves as being so lucky. In my mind though, they were the cool kids. Imagine that . . . religion, better yet Jesus-living was starting to look cool. For those parents who were unable to afford to send their children to a private, Christian-based school, I found myself feeling sorry for them. I wasn't sure why. I think the feelings of regret stemmed from my own dreadful history with public schools. It wasn't necessarily the school or the lack of quality education that made it a painfully frightening time; but perhaps it was my lack of purpose and a sense of belonging as a child with "serious issues."

Either way, I hoped all my friends' parents would chose Lutheran High School; particularly my black friends. I had heard rumors about the school, some good, some not so good. I wondered how I would survive high school with no kids who looked like me. No gospel singing groups, no discussions of the latest hair grease or black hairstyle, no more daring advances toward little white boys who didn't know any better. No, this was high school. Color would become an issue, and at Lutheran there wasn't much of it. Or would there be? Would my time at Lutheran reveal itself to be more like my most memorable experiences at Calvary? Would my first boyfriend be just like Tim, someone who saw beyond my brown skin and kinky black hair? Did Lutheran have dances and proms and weekend bonfires? I had never been to a bonfire. I was overwhelmed just thinking about the many possibilities but totally captivated by the opportunity.

My new friends, the Mackay sisters and a few others were going; mostly white friends—well in fact only white friends, but they were going. We were a family and we were all going. Mom seemed astonished at my decision to go to Lutheran. It was like awaiting the results on election night. Together we had been teeter-tottering across both sides—for and against four years at Lutheran High. On the side "against," social integration would be a major discussion point. Would the lack of diversity inhibit my ability to connect, socialize and perhaps even learn? Would it be so much of a distraction that I would rebel against every good and meaningful thing Lutheran had to offer? In support of the "for" argument would be the many obvious reasons: a consistent exposure to Christian teachings and biblical principles; a smaller student body with unlimited opportunities to excel and participate (there were no tryouts for the volleyball team—*everybody* made the team); and of course there was the race factor. Perhaps the lack of diversity wouldn't be a deterrent at all, but actually a blessing in disguise. Who would I become as a developing, dating young black woman? Would I fancy the only choices I had, or would I disregard my teenage desires and swear to four years of dating isolation? We would rationalize every side, dissecting the ins and outs for the last three months of middle school life.

The Mackays were perhaps the most avid supporters for "life at Lutheran." With two children currently attending the school, they knew the benefits it offered and had hope for what it could do, even for a dysfunctional kid like me. Not only were they hopefuls, they were believers *and* doers. Time and time again they committed themselves to mother and to the manifestation of my destiny.

They would take me to school, sporting events, choir performances—they vowed to do whatever it took to get me there. Mother was anxious at the idea of having to make "Lutheran life" work. The commute was at least 30 minutes and in a pinch . . . she squirmed at the thought of looking to the village to aid in last-minute emergencies. The Mackays ensured mother she need not to worry. They would be there with whatever resources they could muster up to ensure my opportunities were equal and accessible: transportation, study partners and of course, milk—lots and lots of milk.

Before the move to Lutheran High came a move to the neighboring state of Kansas, the city of Lenexa to be precise. Better house, better neighborhood, hopes for a better life. Mother had originally chosen the new residence in anticipation my vote would be to attend high school in the very prestigious Olathe School District. Olathe had diversity, A+ college-bound programs and well over 300 students in what would be my graduating class. Nope, I had chosen Lutheran. My graduating class at Lutheran would be less than 30.

Lutheran High was an interesting place to say the least. A melting pot for sure; filled with a mixture of people, personalities and peer pressures. There was diversity no doubt, but not the kind I was hoping for. It was a diversity of the human race; diversity of the Christian experience. If I were a minority, I was one of many.

What intrigued me most about Lutheran was how this spectrum of people and colorful personas offered virtually the same amount of diversity one would expect in a much larger public school. There were groups and then there were individuals. While the most obvious classification was based primarily on grade level (freshman, sophomore, etc), the classes would soon start to blend—assimilating people and personalities based on common goals, life perspectives and passions.

The groups were pretty standard, characteristic of most high schools—the athletes, the brainiacs, the artists, the performers, the free-spirits and of course the God squad (I'll get to them in a moment). The remaining individuals were independent. These students may have associated with a particular group from time to time, but they were mostly neutral—intentionally so. Most in this group were people confident in their own unique individuality and felt it unnecessary to become committed to any one group. Some were creative minds who refused to be limited to the confines of generalization; a few wore gothic clothes and listened to loud, scary music. Others were loners by default, undue isolation from peers and classmates. In most cases, isolation for the loners was involuntarily. They didn't have a choice. I didn't do well with neglect and abandonment; I would cringe at the thought of people being scorned and rejected—and for what reason? I went out of my way to befriend them—the stutterers, the slow readers, the kids with the tattered clothes. These were *my* people.

What was interesting about the Lutheran groups is at one time or another, I found myself a member of each. I had a smart phase—moments when I thrived on working hard and feeling like I was made of something; something of substance. At the height of my brain phase I would pull all-night study sessions. Mother would beam with joy as she would creep down to my bedroom just after midnight and there I would be, pacing to and fro as though I were a college professor teaching the day's history lesson.

"May," as she so sweetly called me, "don't you think it's time for you to go to bed darlin'? You can do one more final review in the morning . . . you need to sleep."

I wasn't doing it for her to notice, but it meant so much that she did. I was proud she was proud. It would be the fuel to carry me through just one more review of my notes before drifting off to sleep, notebook filled with yellow highlighter markings still in hand.

That moment would become one of many. When I wanted to work, I worked. And when I worked, I toiled. I refused to lose; I despised the thought of failure. Not to mention, I wanted so much to be on the same honor roll bulletin board as the Mackays. They pulled all-nighters too, regularly. After track meets, basketball games or drama rehearsal, they were studying in the dimly lit interior lights of the family minivan.

I loved drama and choir. I would audition for every winter play and the following spring musical. I would never be the lead role, but I had important parts. I wasn't intimidated by my racial disposition. *Sound of Music*, I was a nun. *Pygmalion*, I played a British housekeeper. But in Rodgers and Hammerstein's *Cinderella*, I advanced from my stereotypical "black role." I played the solo-touting Fairy Godmother. This was a big deal—I had gained status. Sure you remember the 1997 television musical *Cinderella*? Whitney Houston embodied the role of the Fairy Godmother. As a senior in high school, I had become Whitney.

"G-O-D . . . yeah you know me!" That was my morning chant as I pranced down the hallways of Lutheran—no fear, no reservations—as a member of the LHS God-squad. My life in the God-squad was more than a moment in time, it was an entire movement. What started as a form of bullying—a humiliating description of the girls and guys who never drank, weren't having sex and had no fun—soon became a badge of honor. I liked being different and was driven by a desire to stand out, so the title never bothered me. It wasn't until I discovered how much more valuable this badge was because of *who* it represented, that I daunted my membership loud and proud "G-O-D . . . yeah you know me!"

While the seeds had been sewn from birth, it was at Lutheran High that I began to discover God. True to most Christian schools, religion—Christian studies to be exact—was one of the core classes of the LHS curriculum. Religion class was exhilarating. I was compelled like a mosquito to water, searching for knowledge, understanding and answers. I refused to believe simply because I was told to believe and the truth was confusing; it was complex. As a teenager struggling to validate her identity and rebelling from the Godly roots from which she stemmed, I wanted to know why I was a Christian. Why should I defend my faith and who was to say it was *my* faith?

I was a modern day Didymus, the man biblically known as Thomas; "Doubting Thomas" is how you may know him. After Jesus had risen from his earthly grave following his crucifixion and death three days prior, Jesus appeared to some of his disciples. Thomas however, was not with them during this first appearance. John 20:25 says,

> *So the other disciples told him, 'We have seen the Lord!' But he [Thomas] said to them, 'Unless I see the nail marks in his hands and put my finger where the nails were, and put my hand into his side, I will not believe it.'*

Indeed, I was Thomas. I attended church regularly, witnessed the faith of my mother and the healing, protecting power of her Savior several times over. But still, I couldn't quite grasp why I believed. I wanted to touch Jesus for myself.

Lutheran would prove I was no match for the teachers and ministers who had dedicated their lives to studying and demonstrating the gospel of Jesus Christ. But these teachers were not like my former public school teachers. Christianity wasn't a contest. They weren't out to win a war with me or even win me over. They were responding to God's call to teach, preach and live the Word of God. They were not put off by my incessant number of questions, unfounded suggestions and accusations, nor my denial that I didn't in fact no as much as

I thought I did. For days, weeks and even years, these teachers would become my spiritual advisors; my ministerial family. They realized the time, teaching and lifestyle witness they invested in me would leave a lasting impression. They were hopeful the seeds they implanted would eventually grow—creating a legacy, a life changed and reclaimed by Jesus Christ.

> *Train a child in the way he should go, and when he is old he will not turn from it.*
>
> *(Proverbs 22:6)*

Coming from Calvary Lutheran I was very familiar with the Lutheran style of worship, bible study and moments of individual reflection. The music was different, worship services seemed almost scripted (they were short and concise—no service lasted more than one hour), and the general tone in which Lutherans reflected on the goodness of God was very solemn, serious business. Lutheran High was much the same. Each week the entire student body gathered for Wednesday chapel service in the school auditorium. Most days, the large factory-like building was cold and drafty. The auditorium was much worse. The seats were old and wooden, and the plastic covering on the large cathedral windows did nothing to keep the air from seeping in. Sometimes it sounded as though the heaters were in overdrive. The clanking of old pipes and the sound of steam racing to reach a frigid and much annoyed student body, often drowned out the sounds of the piano and the blend of teachers and students singing, *Come, thou fount of every blessing, tune my heart to sing thy grace . . .*

As a teenage freshman with certainly better things to do, I remember thinking how the services themselves were less than desirable. Over time and after hundreds of services however, I came to love the feeling that remained when we left that gathering place. The sense of cold and sheer annoyance had nearly vanished by the time service concluded. I couldn't explain it. It wasn't the songs themselves was it? I thought they were long and dry; I never really listened to the words. Perhaps it was the message (not just any words, but God's words), and the way in which these words were delivered that captivated me most. It was though the Savior himself had an audience with me. While most days I searched for any excuse possible to avoid the 30-minute drive to Lutheran; Wednesdays were not that way. Every Wednesday I felt convicted in a way I never was at my foot-stomping, three-hour praising, testimony-raising Church of Christ Holiness.

Was it me or was it them? I loved the Church of Christ Holiness, but why? What *did* I love? Sunday services at my church home were different. They were much livelier, but the feeling, that emotional high that dwelled long after I left the three-story structure with the small but heavenly choir just wasn't the same. Was I Lutheran, was I becoming a Lutheran? What did that even mean? To which movement did I belong?

I'm not soon to forget my days in the free-spirit chapter. This was perhaps the most interesting of all the groups. I imagine my mother was appalled by my saggy bellbottoms, skateboarder shoes, unkempt hair, dark eye shadow and tie-dyed shirts. Black people did not dress this way and certainly didn't present themselves in front of others in this fashion. But I did. During this phase, I reached a point where I simply didn't care. Acne flare-ups were a regular occurrence and my desire to go to school was waning by the weeks.

Ditching school just wasn't an option. I carpooled with the Mackays and by my senior year, the fascination and utter captivation I had with their structured, dreamy milk-filled life was getting on my nerves. They always had their act together, they were always on time, and would bang on my bedroom window when I tried my darndest to skip school. Some days I wanted to do nothing but sleep in. I didn't want to rise to expectations, be all I could be, or achieve the unthinkable. I just wanted to sleep.

The free-spirit chapter was a cloudy time—moments of unclear judgment together with mixed company produced two different lifestyles, two very, very different Merideths. I claimed to live my life one way, worshiped with an unquenchable fire on Sunday, and danced in and out of Godly living every day in between. I had become a master of foolery. Problem was I was fooling no one but myself.

As I became more and more exposed to the world outside of Lutheran, I grew anxious at the thought there was a life I was missing; a life I was being protected from. It was the life of *my people*, my strong, resilient and in some cases, poverty-stricken black people. In my mind, I was being deprived of the ultimate black experience. I had painted the black world as a storybook picture within my mind—a lavish but grossly intense urban life in which people struggled, grinded for good fortune, became parents at a ridiculously young age, and cohabited with baby mamas and baby daddies.

I stereotyped *those* people. They were the people who lived north of 35th and South Benton, hung out in droves on the front porch of the abandoned house on 21st and Prospect, and let their four-year old stay awake until midnight watching music videos on *BET*.

There was no one from *their world* at Lutheran. Yet, I wanted to be so much like them. These weren't people I had read about in newspapers or saw on the 5 o'clock news; they were people I knew. Some of them I merely stumbled on. Lutheran High School sat just ten minutes outside the inner city core of Kansas City. On the days I wasn't carpooling and every night after basketball practice, I was joyriding—looking for *my people*. I was determined to make friends outside of Lutheran; friends who looked like me but didn't share my restrictive bubble of teenage living—teenage living. I was hungry for diversity, attention and personal black connection.

Ok, time for a quick reality check. I know what you're thinking, "Oh no she didn't just say that . . ." Remember, the Christian continuum describes our journey through knowledge, truth and honesty. I suspect at this very moment, you're cringing at the thought I judged and discriminated against my own people. Perhaps you're thinking in disgust, "How haughty of her to refer to black people as *those* people?" Or maybe you're saying to yourself, "Just who does she think she is?"

Or, are you wincing at the thought that at one point in your life, you too have harbored these same feelings—about all types of people—and have never honestly acknowledged and confronted these feelings buried within yourself? My ignorance was my reality.

Gone were the days when I was chasing after dreamy-eyed white boys and trying to fit in at weekend house parties where Lutherans were plenty. This world was perfect but to me, it wasn't real. I couldn't relate. I had everything I could have possibly needed to be successful within arms-reach: a sound education, a reliable network of support, friends and village families, and all the love a mother could muster up; but still it wasn't enough.

Being black at Lutheran High was tough. Although it never seemed intentional, white friends, classmates and teammates would always treat me different. Each morning as I passed them in the hallway, the boys in particular would let out a hype, "Hey what's up homegirl . . . . how's it cookin' home skillet? What good do you know fo sho'?"

"What . . . really?" I would think to myself in utter annoyance. What in the world was a home skillet and why was I being referred to as a kitchen tool? It was as if they wanted me to know they were down for the cause; the black cause.

Social events were no different. From homecoming dances to the annual LHS lock-in, I was expected to know all the latest dance moves, the hottest and oftentimes most vulgar rap songs, and of course the latest hip hop lingo. I was so far from black and it showed, badly. Black wasn't a color, it was a state of being. At Lutheran they implored me for it; desperately seeking to experience the black culture by living vicariously through me. Outside of Lutheran, they shunned me for it; friends at church and even *my people* in the city mocked my white speech and overtly proper disposition.

"You sound like a white girl," they would remark. "You nothin' but an Oreo—black on the outside and white on the inside."

They were right. I was a black-covered Oreo in a sea of Lutheran milk. I needed to get back to black.

Rides through the crime-ridden streets of the 'hood would soon turn into late-night stays and countless lies. My schemes were radicle and unrestrained. Every week I would flash a new story across mother's distressed and overwhelmed mind, explaining profusely how practice had been extended by four hours on Friday nights. My attraction to the streets had become an addiction. Instead of studying I was seducing young men fascinated with my proper speech and naïve sense of innocence. I was their drug of choice, their crack cocaine. I was amazed how every jaunt into the city produced yet another new friend; another opportunity to impress. They were entranced by my presence.

"What you doin' here girl? Where you go to school?" Their intrigue would compel me to flirt further, say something cleverly smart.

"What do you mean I don't belong down here? I'm an independent woman driving my own car." I rolled my eyes with the wit of 30-year old woman, radiating with the immature common sense of a 16 year-old girl.

"I can probably give you a ride if you need one . . ." I would flaunt in jest.

"You know yo' mama goin' be lookin' for you," the stranger would say. ". . . now you know you don't belong down hea'."

As I would let off another bantering but flirtatious, "Whatever . . . ," the stranger would follow after, eventually requesting my phone number and perhaps a date in the very near future. I was black. This was where I belonged.

Mother and I thought we would never reach graduation night. Together we acclaimed the last four years had been the longest of our lives since our time as mother and child. She prayed that I would simply finish high school, and I couldn't wait for my opportunity to escape. A visit to the state university would capture my interest and an insatiable desire to be integrated with people who looked and lived like me. I was going to college.

The summer before going to college I was on my way, or so I thought. I had sampled from the buffet of lifestyles Lutheran had to offer. And while I still wasn't quite sure where I truly belonged or who I was, I was on my way. Unbeknownst to me, it would be this imbalance that would toy with my emotions and potentially threaten all possibilities for a prosperous future.

By day I was focused, I was college-bound; but by night I was restless and craved a life of independence. That summer, it would once again be just she and me—prayerfully putting up with each other for three short months until the time I would finally become independent. In her mind, college would afford a much needed taste of the real world. For me, it boasted a taste of a world untapped. Mother had expectations and I wanted to be free; free of rules, responsibilities and certainly of all restrictions. But mother thrived on rules, she lived by them—curfews, TV restrictions and of course, places I was forbidden to go. And the city, the place that had become my source of refuge and identity was forbidden. Once again, I felt alone. Rules and restrictions made me bitter and rebellious. When mother said don't, I did. When she said stay, I went. I refused to be confined and contained. Four years at Lutheran was long enough and I was ready to live.

I lived alright—in nightclubs, in late night after-parties and in utter defiance of all that was appropriate. I was a bastard child and was determined to act like one. It was undeniable. I was resentful of the fact I didn't have a father—a man in my life to stroke my hair, hold my hand and even scold me like only a father could. When I posed questions to my mother about my father, I soon learned of his whereabouts—where he lived, his type of work and the family he had built outside of me. I recalled meeting him in the gravel driveway of Gran's house in Winnsboro once before when I was about eleven or twelve, but even then I was skeptical of his true identity.

"He couldn't possibly be *my* dad . . ." I thought. There was no way my father would come to see me after twelve years of no communication, pass me a cool $20 bill and then leave again . . . not *my* dad. But he was. That was my dad and all I could remember of him; twenty dollars. No more, no less.

As I was making my last preparations for college, I wrote my dad a letter asking for his love, his time and his help. I wanted a car—I needed a car. As friends and classmates were headed to college, their dads graciously passed on the family Volvo, Toyota, Nissan and Honda. Months prior, mother had given me her car; it was a Honda. But after countless nights of excessive speed and running the Accord until the fuel tank was bone dry—I killed the car. Much like her patience, her tolerance and her gracious spirit, I killed it. So in an act of ungratefulness and self-pity, I wrote my father—demanding his presence and his visibility in my life in the form of a car. I wanted him to pay attention or to pay up; neither happened. My letter went unanswered and my bitterness grew. But mother, heart bruised, gave again—this time it was a Ford Escort. Bitter still, I wanted my father.

Chapter 7

Failing for Two Please

I was pregnant, period. Not kind-of pregnant, maybe-just-a-little pregnant, or even missed-my-period pregnant. I was doubly pregnant. I was seventeen and six months into college, unmarried, away from home and pregnant with twins. My mother was heartbroken and I was tired. I was always tired. Every day was an exhaustive marathon filled with trekking around the ridiculously large campus, ignoring the stares and gossip of girls in disbelief and fighting off sexually crazed campus men who saw me as an easy alternative to the risk of impregnating some promising freshman.

My promise had already been compromised and they knew it, no concerns of defiling me. Pregnancy changed everything and I wasn't ready. I didn't want to be pregnant. Since abortion most certainly wasn't an option, mother and I entertained the possibility of adoption. I cringed at the thought, but danced around the idea with every waking moment. Could I give my children away? Did I have the courage? Or did I secretly resent the truth that I *was* adopted, I *was* given away and I *felt abandoned*? While my ears and mind had received countless reassurances to the adverse, my heart had not. In my heart I was the child no one wanted.

A 200-pound pregnant body, a near-fatal car accident and undeniable feelings of confusion soon brought me home—back to Lenexa with mother. This time for some reason, things were different. I needed her. I was scared and she was hurt yet words of judgment and utter disappointment never surfaced. The next nine months were filled with memories—late nights of ice cream and old movies like *To Sir with Love*, and countless trips to the obstetrician. My experience became her experience. We were emerging as mothers together— she and me.

When the twins were born a sense of great relief consumed us both, only to be followed by a cloud of uncertainty. Here were these two very precious lives— lives I had co-created but we, mother and child, had brought forth together. The risk of failing became the unspoken tension that often threatened to suffocate our very joys.

Always a very determined being, I vowed not to fail. I was sure of it, perhaps unjustifiably arrogant. I refused to fail my children. My first commitment was to establish their identity. Empower them with names full of life, meaning and promise. About the second trimester, when mother and I decided to keep the twins there with us—within the family, a revelation ensued. I finally understood the gravity behind the gift my mother had chosen to birth and her sister promised to protect; the gift that was my life. Eighteen and now a mother myself, these beings—my children, revealed the power and importance of choice.

Evelyn could have chosen to abort me, leave me at the reception desk of a local hospital or place me at the feet of my father before he was willing to care. But she didn't. For whatever reason, she saved me. Betty Joyce would fill the role where she could not. As mother she would preserve my opportunity, the possibility of what could be. She too, would save me. I was humbled; I was honored at the thought. I would name my first born girl after the two women who gave me life. Her name would be Evelyn Joyce.

My son was a vision of hope; the poised posture of an unspoken leader. His face was one of unmistakable strength, much like his great-grandfather Carey. His name would come from Carey's father and the Celtic name meaning, *Young Warrior*. His name would be Evan.

Together they were tiny packages. They were the smallest most fragile beings I had ever seen. I wasn't ready but had no choice. They were mine and I was their mother.

A new mother never forgets her first moments. The worry baby isn't eating enough; the thought she won't wake when he fusses during the night; and the car ride home—the one that feels twice as long even though it is the same unforgettable route that took her to birth new life just a few short days ago.

I wasn't ready, but our village was. As mother and I struggled with crib sheets, baby carriers and the oversized seat belts which seemingly engulfed their fragile little bodies, the doorbell rang. It was Mama Mackay. Night after night she came, she stayed, she sang and she prayed. Whether it was folding blankets, rocking babies as mother and now grandmother napped, or guiding my trembling hand as I attempted to latch baby's mouth to my breast, Mama Mackay remained. One by one the village families surfaced—with gifts, meals, prayers and play toys. I wasn't alone. Mother, Evan, Evelyn and I were not alone.

As my baby weight disappeared so did my interest in being a mother. The newness and fragility of my tiny little packages had become the bane of my existence. I wanted someone else to care, to worry and to pace the floor as teething babies refused to settle. I was selfish and bitter. Their father wasn't there and mother refused to let me sleep. Mornings started at 3 a.m. and days were long. Motherhood was an all-day job and I was working for two. I resented everyone, including my children.

I loved the *thought* of them—gazing at their big brown eyes, stroking their tiny hands and dressing them up in those adorably annoying his and her outfits. But I wanted to pretend. I wanted to play house with them, make them laugh, kiss them lots, read books at night and then disappear along with my permanent "mommy" title. Yet again, I despised my life. I resented the fact I was me.

Looking back it's with a tearful heart I thank God for his unfailing mercy and love despite my desire, better yet, ability to love. I loved no one, not even myself. Today, I marvel at God's willingness to love and care for me in spite of myself. I realize now, in my disobedience God could have removed his hedge of grace from over me—handing me over to a reprobate mind and a destructive heart (Romans 1:28); one that no doubt in selfish pity, could have brought unthinkable harm to two very innocent lives. While I never meant any harm, I provoked it. I just didn't care.

Mother would work every day, supporting the twins, our needs and our broken family. I was unemployed and uninterested—in life, opportunity, even the safety of my own children. When I needed an out . . . I left. I looked for any and every reason to leave the house, to make a quick jaunt to the corner store.

I remember the first time I left them alone. They were napping and we were down to our last diaper. I remember rationalizing with myself for more than an hour . . . how to do it, when to do it, even calculating the time it would take to run to Wal-Mart to purchase the high-priced diapers and drive home. I trembled at the thought but convinced myself I was doing it for them. To take them out in the cold at such a young age would be foolish; and I had no babysitter. No one was there to help so I had no choice. I was convinced of my own selfish lies. I left them that day, and the next day, and the next.

Like an addict I had become enthralled with the brief sensation of freedom coupled with the looming fear that came with leaving. Despite the painful, sinking feeling in my gut as I crept back into the house praying the babies were still ok, it was the unshakable hunger to be unattached that compelled me to leave again and again. I was dancing with God and the devil.

The pattern continued and it grew. Mini-trips to the convenience store when mother was away at work became full fledge escapes out of the back bedroom window; often as late as midnight after mother had finally drifted off to sleep. Each night I scripted my plan, an exit route and even a just-in-case-I'm-caught sob story. In most cases, I did my best to act as selflessly as possible (or so I told myself). I would be courteous enough to put the babies to sleep first, at times even propping up a formula-filled bottle with a pillow ever so gently in their mouths. This would ensure they were fed, full and likely to sleep soundly. On some nights, I would boost the bottle with cereal—a strategy that often guaranteed at least five hours of uninterrupted slumber.

Night after night, the streets would come calling, and I would answer with a devious plan and vigorous execution. Most nights I would return at two or three the next morning to find babies asleep, bottles at their side and mother asleep in her bed. Other nights, I knew I had been discovered. Bottles lie empty on the kitchen counter, soiled diapers lie in a Wal-Mart bag adjacent to the kitchen trash can—evidence a wakened grandmother had tended to the motherless babies throughout the night. On those nights she was waiting—at the door step, sitting in the dark family room, or hovering at the window through which I had crept.

I hated these nights. I didn't want to see her face, her disappointment. Her sorrow-filled eyes made me resent my choice that night. Unfortunately remorse was short-lived. Like a drunk driver racing a freight train, I kept going—planning, escaping and creeping back to the streets for countless nights of unquenchable bliss. Many, many nights I went back.

For twelve months I played Russian roulette with my children's lives—their safety only spared by the grandmother who functioned as the shield between them and me. Not every day was clouded by poor judgment and neglect. I was truly drunk with my own cocktail of misery and misguidance. By night I was fulfilled, my appetite for pleasure was being met which meant by day I was content; filled with joy and temporarily sustained. Like an alcoholic, continual access to my drug of choice made for a happy disposition. Life was good because pleasure was on the way. No longer was motherhood a full-time responsibility, for me it was a daytime production.

The babies couldn't tell the difference, so I thought. I had secured a great job at a local childcare center; the twins' classroom right next to mine. Throughout the day there would be hugs, kisses, waves and games on the playground. After work would be trips to McDonald's, story time at the library and sessions of hide-and-seek at a neighborhood park. But I was drunk, drunk with the idea that my "mommy shift" was almost over. I had given my twins my best, my time, my drunken love.

As I continued along my mystical journey, an enchanting nightlife spent in the streets and in the arms of strange men, one night would destroy my fairy-tale adventure and nearly end my life in the process.

Devious behavior is almost always coupled with haste. Being a sneak requires great stealth, secretive planning and swift movements. Swift movements almost always lead to carelessness and endangerment. I had endangered my children many times before, but in my mind "endangerment" was a relative term.

You see that's the beauty of God's amazing grace; another testament of *who* God really is. Even when we fail to see through the fog of our own ignorance and selfish arrogance, He remains; He waits and then intervenes when necessary. He's a God who empowers his children with freewill and in many cases free-fall. It was my time to fall.

July 24, 2001. It was the day before my twentieth birthday and I was psyched. My teenage days were no more. I had skillfully mastered my practice of sneaking out—leaving babies behind without as much as a creak of the heavy wooden garage door. When I made it out, it was though I had escaped from Alcatraz. I was free. It was as though I had transformed into a storybook superhero—dark mask, mysterious movements; a disguise to hide the real me cowering inside. Everything about me was free. My body and mind were free.

That night I was late. I was always late—for church, for school, heck even for dinner—it really didn't matter. My mother often joked, "Girl, you're going to be late for your own funeral . . . don't you ever care about being on time?"

I didn't.

I was late for my date with my secret nightlife and one very intriguing young man I had become so passionately enthralled with. Shame, I don't even remember his name.

He was on his way to do time, in prison. His crimes unbeknownst to me, I didn't care what he had done. I was his girl and he made sure to let everyone know. I was a prize piece within his urban trophy case. I was an outsider and he liked that, we both did.

All morning I rehearsed the story, the lie I would ever so eloquently impress upon my mother. After numerous "I'm sorry" and "I swear on everything I love, I won't do it again" promises, mother was done. She had reached her limit.

It was like clockwork—every hour on the hour—I was telling my story, begging and pleading for mother to allow me to leave that night. I explained how I thought I was doing the right thing by asking her in advance; normally I disappeared like vapor in the night. Wouldn't my consideration, my courtesy to ask in advance count for something?

I was selfish, but I didn't know it. My requests resembled more of impractical demands rather than respectable, reasonable appeals. I had no basis for roving the streets night after night—there was nothing respectable and reasonable about it.

When she wouldn't budge, my temporary moment of civility was gone. I was furious. I hated feeling rejected, refused. I was like a toddler who couldn't have her way—but I was a mother, not a toddler. I didn't care.

Again, my tenacity for surreptitious planning sprang into action. I was going out and no one was going to stop me. Hours of prep time ensued—hair, makeup, clothes were perfect. Babies were content in their playpens and I was on my way. This time though, there was daylight to contend with. Everyone was awake, alert and aware. It was as though God himself, together with his band of angels had roused everyone for vigilant duty, mother and babies alike.

How was I going to get out now? My plans were thrown as well as my confidence. I was nervous, but undeterred. I would have to confront them—mother, babies and all; me, she and them face-to-face with my lies.

"Where do you think you're going?" She bellowed from atop the stairs. I was only inches away from the front door (seeing how the standard garage egress was no longer an option).

"I told you . . ." I whined softly in quiet defense. I knew raising my voice would only jeopardize my plans.

"I have to help my friend move. You don't know them. They're going away for school and most likely won't come back to Missouri—this is really important to me."

There it went; another untruth without as much as an eye-blink. This was more than a poker face, it was a poker life. Even I didn't know who I was.

Back and forth, the debate continued as the twins played quietly in the upstairs bedroom, alone. She wasn't budging. I was losing the battle—my white flag soon to rise in surrender.

After thirty minutes, both sides relentless and my perfectly applied makeup starting to sweat, I gave in. She had won. The twins were coming with me.

I was furious but was determined to remain focused. With every possible profanity spewing from my lips I quickly dressed the twins, hurled some his and hers Onesies into a bag and tossed everything into my Jeep—twins, bag and all.

As mother stood peering from the perch of her second-story bedroom window, I peeled out as fast and as loud as I could. If anything were to happen tonight, particularly to the twins, I wanted her to know . . . it was her fault; I did this because of her.

With my destination being over 25 miles (a 40-minute drive) from Lenexa city limits, I drove fast, death-sentence fast. It wasn't until I entered the on-ramp at Interstate 435, glancing momentarily into my rear-view mirror to see tiny twin bodies bopping loosely about, that I realized what I had done. Driving 90 miles per hour my babies were unprotected—from unpredictable elements on the highway, from reckless driving both in and outside our Jeep, and from me. They were unrestrained; abandoned car seats rolling to and fro in the truck's tailgate.

The brief but terrified glance wouldn't be enough. I kept going, seemingly faster, as if I was expecting or preparing for something awful to happen. It was as though I knew something was coming.

Swerving in and out of lanes I was becoming increasingly frustrated, swelled with anxiety at the realization I was late and had nowhere to leave the children. It seemed like forever, driving down the highway glancing to the digital clock before me and the very petrified children behind me. They knew something was wrong.

My reckless haze was broken when a small round figure emerged without warning from the back seat, grazing the long silver earring that dangled from my right ear. It was Evan's ball falling suddenly to the floor—directly into the path of my accelerator. I reached for it quickly.

As I struggled to make contact with the ball my eyes left the road, my complete and focused attention now on retrieving the ball.

It wasn't until the ball rolled ever so slowly away from my outstretched hand that I realized what was happening, I was swerving.

I jerked up to find my car, now at a cruising speed of 95 miles per hour, just inches away from making contact with the white sedan in front of me. The driver must have been startled at the sight of my car approaching hers with no evidence of slowing, she braked. She braked hard.

Following suit I slammed on my breaks in attempts to avoid thrusting the Jeep and all that was contained within through the front windshield. It was too late.

The car jerked in response as though it was possessed, to the left and to the right it went. Swerves turned to circles, we were spinning. After two complete turns I stopped counting. As we circled out of control I went numb. We were going to die.

Perpendicular to the oncoming traffic, we had spun from the outer left lane across the four-lane highway. In its final spin the car quickly straightened. Now on a bridge; a row of cement highway barriers lie straight ahead. I braced myself for impact. Barriers and I would collide—head on.

BAM!

The sound of the airbags erupting and the large steel frame striking the concrete blocks was deafening. It was like an explosion. Bright orange flames followed by a thick plume of black smoke burst from under the hood of the shattered vehicle. Kicking and screaming soon turned to sheer panic as I found myself trapped in the front seat of the burning wreckage. Trying both the driver and passenger doors, I suddenly remembered the babies. The twins were in the back seat and they hadn't made a sound.

With my heart, lungs and stomach in my throat I turned reluctantly, praying my eyes would be graced with a miracle, Evan and Evelyn spared.

What I saw was an image, a moment in time that will remain with me forever. There were my children, the seedlings which I bore, curled into a fetal position on the floor—one on each side—tucked ever so gently in the foot spaces behind the driver and passenger seats.

Have you ever experienced such a moment? It's a brief lapse in time in which you're not quite sure or even believe perhaps what your eyes are seeing. It was as though the children had been bundled, tucked and held by the right and left hands of God.

It is only now, thirteen years later I have come to realize and embrace that moment. At the time I was only relieved, thankful that beyond the conviction of reckless driving, I had escaped from being charged for manslaughter one and two.

Realizing the babies were unscathed I lunged into the back seat, scooped them into my arms and hurried out of the sweltering vehicle. I was fine. We had survived. Losing nothing more than a single shoe (imagine the impact, so much so as to remove the very shoe I was wearing), we walked away unharmed. The car was totaled.

I missed the going-away celebration that night but escaped with my life, our lives. Surely, I thought my days of dancing with the devil were over. I was sorely mistaken. After the accident my unruly escapades slackened but they certainly didn't cease. Shortly after losing my first and only job, I lost all hope—again. Like most Christians at some point along their continuum, I found myself truly remorseful for the wrong I had done. I had hurt my mother to the core and thoughtlessly jeopardized the well-being of my children. I was entrusted to their care and I was failing. I was failing Evan and Evelyn.

If this wasn't bottom, I didn't know what was. I regretted my poor decisions and yearned for a contrite heart. In all my searching, I had yet to find it. I wanted to know how it felt to at least *want* to change. I felt much like Paul when in Romans 7:14-24 he expressed his anguish and painstaking frustration with his inability to control the ongoing conflict between the right he desired to do and the sin, by nature he was destined to commit:

> [14] *We know that the law is spiritual; but I am unspiritual, sold as a slave to sin.* [15] *I do not understand what I do. For what I want to do I do not do, but what I hate I do.* [16] *And if I do what I do not want to do, I agree that the law is good.* [17] *As it is, it is no longer I myself who do it, but it is sin living in me.*
>
> [18] *I know that nothing good lives in me, that is, in my sinful nature. For I have the desire to do what is good, but I cannot carry it out.*

In one of my many brief but surreal moments of remorse I decided to begin the journey toward independence. Mother and I agreed my unpardonable behaviors and lack of responsibility were more than the two of us could deal with—especially under one roof. I moved out; unemployed, no prospects, no direction, no clue.

This would be the last flight from the protective nest in Lenexa. I was leaving with my babies and bags in hand—this time no boys or late-night bashes to hurry to. I was headed for my newly leased Section 8 apartment, confident that this time would be different. I was ready to be on my own. It was just us three—Evan, Evelyn and me.

As seasons changed and the twins grew to become toddlers, the separation from mother proved to be a good move. When no one else was around to play mom and dad, responsibility and maturity weren't optional. We had built a cozy home in our small but warm two bedroom apartment. We had two couches, a kitchen table, a few toys and a couple of mattresses. Mother offered some more substantial accommodations—a dresser, actual bed frames, but we had no money and no means of acquiring and moving the pieces. We would manage with our modest furnishings, our minimal monthly budget of foods stamps and our mattresses. It wasn't much, but it was home.

The kids and I did everything together. We learned to embrace and look forward to the simplest of pleasures—from stove-boiled hot dogs to playing kickball at the apartment complex playground. Whereas I never cooked at mother's house in Lenexa, *I* was now the mother and I cooked every night. Macaroni and cheese was unfortunately a constant at every meal, but every night there was a meal—a meal with milk.

Not only were there meals, but every night seemed to be movie night. Having managed to salvage a few Disney favorites from our previous home in Lenexa, *Cinderella* was by far our most cherished treasure. When dinner was done and dark had set, there was something very calming and almost surreal about watching the silver sparkly palace unfold on the pitch black TV screen (the trademark opening of Walt Disney films). It was though for a moment we were in a world of make believe—Cinderella's world. It was a fairytale with a happy ending; a beautiful castle, talking animals as friends and Prince Charming. In "Cindy's world" everything was going to be alright.

I wanted so much for things to be alright, but they weren't. While my mommy routine became more and more the norm, I began to get more and more restless . . . again. Each night I watched and listened as twenty—and thirty somethings passed in and out of the apartment complex—weekend attire, nightclub dresses and heels, music beating and Jay Z blasting—and I was at home; home with babies.

I yearned for the life of an independent woman—free of children, cares, sexual inhibitions and certainly spiritual restrictions. But I wasn't. I was a young mother—unwed, unattractively tied to the baggage no man wanted. I was twenty-one and unwanted.

Sin is ridiculous. It's destructively and unfairly ridiculous. Sin is an awful condition, a lifestyle that cripples and corrupts the most decent of people; a natural and inherited cancer that only Jesus Christ can cure. It is the barrier that keeps us from God and prevents us from exercising the very desires of our Heavenly Father's heart; desires such as love, faithfulness, kindness, patience and forgiveness *(Romans 8:8)*.

Sin often fosters a mental and emotional handicap in which we become blind to truth and the real meaning of holiness. Using devices such as greed, jealously and deceitfulness, sin causes us to think, say and do things we were never created to do. We were made to please and worship God our Father in every aspect of our lives *(Revelations 4:11, Isaiah 43:7).*

I hate sin . . . now. At twenty-one I didn't, and didn't know I needed to. In fact, I worshiped sin. I didn't realize it is humanly impossible to conquer sin and its many tactics and traps. Without the saving power of Jesus Christ and the forgiveness that comes with accepting Him as Lord of my life, sin would always have reign over me—my words, my thoughts and my actions. I was a slave to sin *(Romans 6:20).*

It was sin that led me to look longingly toward the window, devising ways in which to abandon my children for a night of pleasure. It was sin that dared me to bring strange men into my apartment to play father to my children because I needed someone to love me for me. And it was sin that drove me to lie and to steal—money, food, credit cards—whatever I deemed necessary to survive. My sin became my life. My life was enslaved by sin.

I cannot lie. That apartment that once symbolized a place of freedom, refuge and restoration for the family of three soon became a dark, dreadful prison filled with horrible days and long painful nights. I left my children in that prison, night after night, after night. Alone they stayed. Hallways blocked by couches and chairs, I tucked them in at night and packed them in tight—night after night, after night.

I chased men, one in particular. He was a music industry phenomenon and I was his pet wagging closely behind. I chased after him as my children longed after me. He abused and disregarded me just as I was neglecting and rejecting them. The further he strayed, the more I pursued. The hope of a husband, a father for my children and a jumpstart to my lifelong dream of becoming a worldwide singing sensation—he was my Prince Charming. I prayed he had come to take me away. Instead, he left, he cheated and he continued to stray. I trusted him and so wanted to please him. Every day I gave him all of me—my car, my body, my very integrity as a woman and what little money I had was at his disposal. Each night I would cook, a painstaking sacrifice made in hopes my wife-like measures would keep him there with me. After a day of doing God knows what with the resources I provided, he would come home and eat with us. We would eat as a family. I would tell my small unsuspecting children,

"Daddy's home, Daddy's home!" He wasn't Dad, but they didn't know the difference.

We'd watch Cinderella together, my magical night was complete. I could never fully relax though, as I found myself nudging closer and closer slipping my head under his broad shoulder and the outstretched arm embracing me. I tucked myself in tight hoping he would feel my heart beating against his chest—a sign I *needed* him to stay right there with me. I couldn't bear the thought of him leaving. When he left I cried. I imagine when I left, the twins cried too.

One night I had had enough. I was tired of being left alone there in that cold dark apartment, just them and me. I was leaving to find him. I fed the children, bathed them and tucked them away into the pallet of blankets that lie on their bedroom floor. As they drifted to sleep, I kissed their foreheads and whispered a prayer. It would be the last prayer I prayed in the prison that night,

> *. . . I know God, I know. But not today. Just protect them, watch over them and keep them in Your arms tonight. Tonight is the last time. I promise, this is the last time . . . Amen*

I didn't look back as I crept out of the apartment. I closed the door and walked away.

I was determined to find him, the man who was breaking my heart; the one who refused to stay. I called the only friend I had—a girl who had become my partner in sin. Together we were favorites at bars, clubs and private parties. I was the quiet one—scared, out of place, looking for love. She was the one they loved. She didn't look for them, the men always came looking for her.

We arrived to a familiar spot in a trendy social district in the city. It seemed like everyone was out that night. In my mind all I could think of was him and the babies. If I could find him, I could get home to my babies. I needed him at home where he belonged.

Time was dragging. It seemed like forever and still I hadn't found him. I knew he would be there, he was always there. That was his spot, it was our spot. It was the same place at which he and I first met—he giving me a "pssst . . . hey beautiful can I talk to you," and me flirtatiously ignoring him in gest. It was here he promised to make me his wife; I would travel the country with him— me and the babies. I was coming to retrieve my man and my promise. I refused to leave without them.

My heart went cold as I approached our cherished place, gazing into the window in front of me. There he was with her, a strange face climbing about him, kissing his face and neck, pouncing about him like a dog in heat. She was defiling my love, my heart's very happiness and the man I thought was mine.

My eyes swelled and I jerked away quickly, pretending I didn't see a thing.

"Is that . . ." my friend interrogated as she flung herself around to face me, probing in disbelief.

"—don't say his name, I scolded. "Don't you dare say his name to me!"

A tear fell, and then another. My fairytale was over.

I hated him, I hated love. I was ready to leave. I would flee toward home as fast as I could. I was ready to curl into ball with my babies. I would bury myself in the blankets on the floor, me and the babies who loved me.

Making our way through the crowd of drunken party goers, I realized I was alone. A broken heart simply can't see the world through the cracks and open wounds. The life, the music, the smiling faces were all a blur. I was wandering through crowds of people, yet walking alone.

But she wasn't ready to go. She loved to party, to drink and to dance. Although I had been rejected and publically humiliated, I was determined to accompany my friend—because that's what friends are for; I wanted to ensure at least one of us had a good time.

As the night progressed my resistance to indulge in the world around me weakened; one drink, then another, and another. That night my lips were tainted by fermented drinks from every color of the rainbow—yes, even brown.

I was never one to drink before. I was a suburban girl from Lenexa whose ears were graced with songs from Lutheran hymnals and whose glasses where always filled with milk. I had seen what alcohol could do when limits were reached and surpassed; thinking to myself how stupid one looks when drunk beyond her wits.

But tonight I was that one, the stupid girl who fell for the stupid lies of stupid Satan.

That night I danced like it was nobody's business. Tina Turner had nothing on me. I loved to dance; it was so liberating. Mixed with a few shots of Barley and rum, the uncontrolled yet rhythmic movement of my body made me forget the night's woes and calamities. I quickly forgot about my bruised ego . . . and my babies. Oh my God, the babies.

Since the abandonment of my children was such a closely guarded and very dark secret, I gently but repeatedly nudged my friend telling her it was time to go.

As we stumbled toward the parking lot—she drunken and dazed, me sick with worry and fear—we found ourselves stopped again, this time by a couple of men, thug-looking men.

—If I may digress, it's amazing how once we've made up our mind, whether in life or in deciding to choose a Christ-like path, Satan does all he can to divert us from our course. He uses any and all devices; the most powerful weapons he has. Further, I'm convinced he never ever plays fair. But of course, he's the father of all deceit. As if attacking *God's* children isn't enough, he takes the low blow, packing his punch with the thing, the addiction or the person mostly likely to deter us from doing what's right; it's his own anti-Christ kryptonite.

My weakness was the fatherly facade that seemed apparent in most men. I was easily fooled by their slick talk, athletic physique and the cash they flashed when everyone was watching. Oh to be loved by a man.

Whenever she and I went out, I knew my role and she had hers. An interesting role-play, almost as though it was rehearsed. I was the smart one, the well-spoken wallflower and she—well, she was noticeable. Her outspoken personality was as large as her bodily assets, the ones men drooled over. I was pretty but she had the body. Next to her I was invisible—mind, mystery and all.

As she proceeded to flaunt herself toward one of the men, I noticed his eyes—a perfect complement to the green and white Astros jersey that draped his six-foot-four-inch frame. He was attractive, a dark-skinned stallion resembling a cross between a professional football player and a Crenshaw gangster up to no good. I was memorized.

As my eyes continued to gaze him over ever so conspicuously, I noticed a hint of disinterest as he made eye contact with her only momentarily, then quickly refocused on the glowing cell phone clutched tightly in his hand. He was there for something, perhaps waiting on someone, but not her.

As my mind raced, my heart still aching, I played back the events of the night realizing it was girls like her that made it impossible for women like me. I had fought for my love, cooked for my love, even neglected my maternal responsibilities to chase after him. That was it. I wasn't going to lose another prospect to her—the promiscuous woman's flirtatious and provocative shenanigans. There was only one way to get his attention, play drunk.

As best as I could I stumbled and slurred words, moving slowly but attentively towards him. He was looking directly at me. Gently grabbing his muscular bicep toward my chest I whispered, "Do you know what he did to me today? Let me tell you what he did . . ." He could hear the pain in my voice.

His eyes locking tightly with mine, I felt my whispered words turning into tears. Emotions were setting in; I had to keep it together.

"What did he do to you babe . . ." he inquired now facing full frontal towards me.

The way he beckoned for my response made me weak. He asked as though he already knew the answer. He knew I didn't belong there.

His compassion empowered me, turning my staggering stance into a hostile rant. As I recalled my night's tragedy he too became concerned—for me and for our safety. "Let me get you home babe, I'll put you in a cab . . . you don't need to be out here."

Bantering back and forth a bit longer, I pretended to ignore his gentle pleas just to hear him insist on our departure once more—

"Ok, I'll leave if you insist."

"Well, how will I know if you made it home safely?" His persistence was beyond endearing.

"I'll give you my number . . . but it's only for tonight," I dared. "I really don't know you like that so don't lock it in your phone or nothin'."

He laughed as we exchanged numbers. Placed in a cab, I headed home.

With a newfound hope that perhaps true love wasn't unreachable, I was settled in my mind, everything would be alright. It was time to slow down—making it work with just me and the kids. I needed to fix a few things before I entertained the thought of a new mate. I made up my mind, tonight would be the last time I would ever leave them alone.

The breaking of dawn beat me home. The children always woke at the first hint of sunrise. It was almost 6:30 when I turned the corner entering the corridor leading to my apartment building. My fantasy soon turned into an overwhelming sense of fear. There standing at my front door were two police officers and a Sherriff.

As I slowly shifted the gear into park my body shook in utter horror and disbelief. I didn't know whether to drive away or flee on foot. The officers had seen me, neighboring parents standing in utter disbelief at their side. There was nowhere to run.

Where they injured? Were they burned? Had they wandered off . . . were they dead? My mind was scattered with calamitous thoughts. I wanted to die. I deserved to die.

What ensued over the next two hours included a series of questions, interrogation, discovery and looks of shame from the building's landlord and neighbors. I had abandoned my children and my secret was out. Evan and Evelyn had been found wandering the complex playground in their pajamas and bare feet. They crawled in-between the couch and chair barrier I so methodically arranged the night before, unlooked the door and adventured into the world outdoors. A neighbor who saw them roving alone brought them into her house, fed them and called the police.

There in my apartment I retorted with the maneuvers I knew best; I wept sorely, blamed an absent father—both theirs and mine—and begged pity from disapproving single mothers who stood watching in total disgust.

I felt like the woman brought before Jesus in the temple court who had been caught in the act of adultery (John 8:2-11). I imagine the woman didn't just walk toward the Savior voluntarily, but was dragged by the Pharisees as they flung her at the feet of Jesus who stood solemnly at the front of the outdoor sanctuary.

The Pharisees cried,

> [4] . . ."*Teacher, this woman was caught in the act of adultery.* [5] *In the Law Moses commanded us to stone such women. Now what do you say?*" [6] *They were using this question as a trap, in order to have a basis for accusing him.*
>
> *But Jesus bent down and started to write on the ground with his finger.* [7] *When they kept on questioning him, he straightened up and said to them, "Let any one of you who is without sin be the first to throw a stone at her."* [8] *Again he stooped down and wrote on the ground.*

I had been caught in my sin and the world was watching; my babies in the protective custody of the police and me in handcuffs. They were taking me away. I was being detained not for my sin of neglect, but for failing to pay an outstanding speeding ticket. I had a warrant, I was going to jail.

When mother arrived to the apartment she didn't say a word. The look of utter dismay caused her gentle face to droop. She was exhausted. Her spirit was tired and her trusting heart was tattered from abuse. She had come to retrieve the children. They would be released to her indefinitely.

The ride to the municipal jail was long and hot. I felt as though I was watching a scene from *Law and Order: Criminal Intent* play out before me as my body slid and slipped in the back of the white police van. The handcuffs were tight; they bruised my hands and tarnished my soul. I felt the very life deflating from within me.

Two hours passed and no rescuer in sight. I cried so much my eyes were nearly swollen shut and my head racked with gut-wrenching pain. I would get a single phone call, but who would I call? Who would I share my darkest secret with? And once my secret was revealed, would they look at me the same or would they reject me in absolute disgust like the onlookers outside my apartment door?

Mustering what little energy I had, I slowly pierced the lids of my heavy-laden eyes. As I looked toward the ceiling an image came to mind—the burly black man who tucked me oh so securely in a cab just a few hours before. My fingers trembled uncontrollably as I dialed the numbers.

"Tikko . . . it's Merideth. Can you come and get me?" Silence on the other end of the line.

Waiting for Tikko in the cold dark cell was sobering. What once were a mother's gentle hands were now the restricted arms of a selfish, yet unequivocally scared teenage girl. The sharp metal against my depressed limp body made me think of the women inmates I had seen on TV. I cringed at the reality my body was not my own. I was an aggressor, an unpredictable threat; the iron bars were proof.

Thirty minutes later the handcuffs were gone. Exhausted with grief my eyes closed once more. In the back seat I lay curled like a baby in her mother's arms; I fell into a deep sleep as he drove off. I was rescued in the arms of Tikko.

Chapter 8

Torture and Turning Points

When I lost the twins, I was sure I had hit rock bottom. I couldn't bear the thought of a greater loss, but wasn't quite sure why the thought troubled me so. Was it because I truly was experiencing a great loss or was it because I had been exposed? I was caught. The fact was I had neglected the only two beings who cared not of my past, my faults nor my false motherly façade. They knew me as mother.

After being released from jail I was in a state of confusion and undoubtedly in need of an intervention. Mother was now untouchable. The lifeline I had so long misused and had taken for granted was gone. The children were removed from my custody and given to her care. I was forbidden to contact mother or the children in any form. I had become the modern-day, self-exiled prodigal son. I was one of *those* cases. I was forever in the welfare system, the world would know I was a mother of neglect; I had brought this on myself.

Unlike the prodigal son, the state of Missouri had provoked my right to return home. In my state of disarray I bunked with my new boyfriend. Tikko and I stayed with his friends in the inner city—on the corner of 31st and South Benton. I most definitely wasn't in Kansas anymore.

Night after night I searched—my mind, my history, any places and situations in which I recalled feeling safe and secure. Truth be told there were countless times, places and people that came to mind, most of which were reflective of moments within my village. I could run to my village. But safety and security were not my sole priorities. The devil would not allow those to be the only conditions I considered.

As I pondered, he whispered, "Who is less likely to judge you?"

"You don't need to be lectured, you've been through hell. You're in hell" he taunted.

"Your family, those *Christians* in your family, they'll beat you down with Bible verses and backlash . . . you don't need that. Where is God now?" he contended with a vile satisfaction.

The devil was right. I didn't need that and I refused to hear it. I was in hell and no one was going to tell me any different. I was the victim. And who was God to me now? He couldn't possibly love me and probably couldn't stand the sight of me. I had hurt Him terribly, I knew it. God didn't know me; I was a stranger in His eyes.

So instead of safe and secure, I searched for the one memory that offered a sense of protection. I needed someone who would understand and embrace my life choices, who would empathize with my loathing sense of self-pity and who would protect me from the big bad world. I would stay right there with Tikko.

Living with Tikko was an experience unlike any other. His life was grimy, messy almost. He came from a world where people hustled, struggled to survive and thrived on the camaraderie that was the 'hood. In the 'hood you didn't enter a room without speaking to everyone present; to do so was a sign of disrespect.

In the 'hood people worked hard—whatever their occupations—some legal and some not. They toiled long hours during the day and let their hair down at night. Every night was a celebration of *I made it through*—a hard day's work, another day of getting money, the danger of the streets. In some parts of the 'hood people celebrated the simple fact they survived. *Today I didn't encounter a bullet with my name on it.*

After a few weeks the 'hood was home. Forbidden to contact the only family I had ever known, Tikko was my family. Together we were man and woman surviving together. By this time I had come to know Tikko intimately, his tendencies, personality traits, foods he liked to eat and the nuances that drove him crazy. I had studied everything about him and together we exchanged stories of our pasts and the breaking points that had driven us to our present.

Tikko was a father of two and coming out of a broken relationship with a woman who was a mother like me—really not a mother at all. He had been raised by his grandmother and grandfather, devout Jehovah's Witnesses who embodied the religion in every sense of the word. On many nights Tikko would tell me countless stories of when his grandmother would lock the front door when he broke his ten 'o clock curfew or when she would jump on the phone when he was attempting to court the likes of a young lady,

"Get off the phone with that harlot!" She would rage. "You know Jehovah doesn't like them loose women!"

Feeling entrapped within the compound, which literally consisted of a ten-foot fence around the perimeter of his grandparents' property, Tikko set out as an independent man. He was fifteen and on his own, nurtured only by friends, drug dealers, scattered family members and the life that was 'the streets.'

Unsurprisingly, Tikko's life became the streets. Forced to defend a mother struggling with a drug addiction and a father whose presence was spotty at most, he loved his family—his grandparents and both his parents. He knew they loved him. But still, they weren't there, not like a man of fifteen needed them to be. The streets were his only family.

Tikko was masterful in the way he lived and thrived. Zealous with an entrepreneurial spirit, Tikko worked hard, but on his own terms. When we met his resume read *Hustlers-R-Us*, his occupation—to get customers what they needed, what they wanted. He was the medicine man and patrons looked to him to get their pleasure of choice.

I was fascinated by his work, the covert and ambiguous nature of it. I knew when transactions were going down: the phone would ring, he'd take the call from the other room—a conversation no more than five minutes long, and then off we went to an unfamiliar house to meet an unfamiliar person. They were unfamiliar to me but they were his clients.

Whenever a 'job' came calling, Tikko insisted I tagged along. He never left me behind; he was proud I was his girl. Soon, the two of us were spotted everywhere—he and I together. Like peanut butter and jelly, friends around the 'hood got accustomed to the tag-team duo, Tikko and Merideth.

With Tikko I was living a life not my own. I was free in every respect—finding my identity, living out a single, child-free existence and wandering through a social melting pot, one I never knew existed. Life was good, relatively speaking. Although I hadn't spoken to the children in months, I knew they were in good hands. This was the time to get myself together, live the life I was itching to live, all the while knowing one day I would have to return to my duty as a mother. *That* was my life, there was no escaping it.

Tikko's friends were a constant in our lives. He was a neighborhood socialite; he knew everyone and everyone knew Tikko. His cadre of friends represented a blend of all things worldly—couples, lesbian lovers, blacks, whites, rappers and preachers. I was intrigued by them all.

While all the friends were good-natured and no doubt exciting to observe, there was one couple that always seemed to command center stage—Sterling and Shiloh. When they were good they were good, when they were off and things were bad, they were toxic. Everything about their relationship seemed disturbing to me. Loving each other one moment and fist-fighting the next, I had never witnessed such a rollercoaster ride of emotions.

On many nights I watched in utter horror, after hours of the couple's alcohol and marijuana binging had ensued, the dynamic between Sterling and Shiloh went from kissing passionately on the couch to exchanging profanities and hurling full bottles of Corona at each other's heads. I was petrified when they came around, but my Tikko was the intercessor. He would intervene, reminding them of why they were together even now, after years of fighting and making up. They would come together, hug and coexist in a somewhat cordial fashion until the next brawl erupted. I was still convinced, they were crazy.

Being exposed to such foreign and in many cases crude elements, my tolerance for all that was decent, right and appropriate quickly diminished, frankly disappeared. Here I was again, going places I had no business going and mirroring the life of fictional female characters I had seen played out on TV. I was Bonnie and he was my Clyde. Our lives were a mimicking role-play of theirs.

Although I had finally landed a job, it paid minimum wage and extra money was nearly impossible to come by. Since Tikko had no transportation of his own, I financed us a car—a used piece of a junk from a hole-in-the-wall dealership that required you to sell your soul just to maintain the payments. Before Tikko, I did anything to survive. I wrote bad checks for groceries and kid's meals from Sonic™, took cash advances in amounts almost three times my biweekly salary, and even stole credit card numbers out of my mother's wallet when she wasn't looking; I used her credit to make sure I could eat.

After meeting Tikko my devious behavior only grew. Now there were two of us in need, in debt and desperate to find temporary fixes for systemic issues—we were broke and disconnected from anyone and anything spiritual in nature. Like all couples, our relationship had its highs and lows, both of which were further exasperated simply because of the very environment in which we lived. Tikko and I had never fought like Sterling and Shiloh though. We fussed, yelled and even engaged in a bout of inappropriate name calling, but we never fought to hurt each other, especially not physically. At least I thought . . .

There is something about the way the human brain catalogs certain memories—birthdays, anniversaries, first kisses and unforeseen deaths—they all have a unique and unforgettable file. In most cases, it's not the event itself that becomes engraved in our minds and leaves a permanent scar upon our human spirit, but it's the sensory activities associated with those events—it's the sounds we heard, the smell in the air and the sights we couldn't forget; these are the things that make the memories truly unforgettable.

I never will forget our first fight. While the recollection of what was said, what drove us to the point of no return remains to be a vague and no doubt irrelevant issue, the memory of what happened next will never die.

He hit me. And it wasn't one of those girly shoves, the kind where you can tell he really wants to hit you but knows better. Tikko beat me, fist balled tight in utter outrage and disgust. It was though the devil himself was trying to kill me; I had never seen him so angry.

Ok, so I had an attitude, I knew I did, but that's what made us click. We were two hot-heads too good to be told anything. I would get in his face and he would get in mine. But that's where we drew the line. We spoke in anger, but never acted on it. Physical violence was the unspoken boundary we knew never to cross.

It was one punch, directly to eye. I blacked out as I fell to the ground on the front lawn of the compound—his grandmother's house. As I came to, still disoriented from the collision with my boyfriend's hand, I froze in horror and disbelief. Was I too embarrassed to move or was I still in shock? I couldn't believe the man with whom I entrusted my life and safety had struck me. In my mind he could do no wrong. He was my fortress, the very lifeline who met the needs and unforeseen challenges of each new day. But he hurt me, I didn't know this man. My trust in him was forever broken.

While I remember the blow all too well, I remember the world around me perhaps even more—how time stood still, how people watched, how the dog across the street barked incessantly at a very high and annoying pitch, and how his grandmother the self-proclaimed woman of 'Jehovah' stood there, she just stood there. My face was bludgeoned to the point of being unrecognizable, but my spirit was permanently crushed. The next two hours were a blur. As I cleaned my face, cowering fearfully in his grandmother's bathroom, family members one after the other attempted to calm Tikko down, but the line had been crossed; we'd never be the same.

With my mind and emotions composed as best as possible, I slowly reached for the door hoping Tikko had gone. I walked swiftly to my car, only to find him driving away with her, his children's mother; she had come to rescue my hero. That night I lost on two fronts—my man and my integrity were gone.

I had no man, no protector, nowhere to go. I found myself on the front step of the one person Tikko and I had grown to trust—his father Otis. When he opened the door his face said it all, his sorrow-filled eyes positioned themselves as to say, "Oh Lord, I knew this would happen. Why did he hurt this little girl . . . ?"

Otis took me in, iced my swollen face and prepared a pallet on his couch where we talked for hours. When my heart couldn't relive the night's events any longer, he kissed my forehead and tucked me in. I thanked Otis for being my father that night.

The next morning I drove to mother's house. Worried about what her response would be, I hoped she would say nothing. I wanted her to open the door, let me in and assure me everything would be ok. She could assure me by simply saying nothing.

The familiar lump in my throat returned once more. It was the same feeling I felt the night of the car accident and the morning I lost the twins, it was a rich mixture of anxiety, nausea and sorrow. I had done wrong, but I wanted to come home.

When she opened the door, her expression was much like Otis'. Her grief was deep, her sunken face showing signs of exhaustion. Caring for the twins full-time was something a twenty-some mother should do, not a sixty-something. Her spirit couldn't take any more, but her heart bled deeply for her only child who stood before her battered and displaced.

She proceeded to ask me why I was there; she unwaveringly affirmed, "You know you can't be here . . . we are not going to violate the protection order. If you stay they will take your children for good . . . Merideth, you have to leave."

She closed the door, I walked away. Death looked more and more appealing. I was sure I had nothing more to live for.

Today when we reflect on the memory of that morning, she assures me just how difficult that moment really was. I explained how I felt so abandoned, as though I was to blame for my beaten exterior. She looks at me, eyes locking with mine, trying her best to hold back a flood of tears she replies,

"You don't know how it hurt me to see *my* child, my baby standing at the door, face beaten black and blue. I didn't know what to say and there was nothing, absolutely nothing I could do."

Her voice trembles, "That man had beaten my baby and all I could do was pray. Looking back, I didn't know what would have happened had I allowed you to stay. We could have lost those babies . . . we had to do what was best for them."

"I know mom," I reply with eternal gratitude.

Someone had to be mom and protect the ones who couldn't protect themselves. I was distraught at the time; but I knew why she did what she did.

Pandora's box was opened, but I was determined to stand firm. I refused to be walked on, mistreated and abused. I was no one's punching bag, particularly not any man's. I was not this woman depicted in *Lifetime* movies and daytime dramas. I was not a woman whose boyfriend beat her. I refused to be.

The next two years were rocky. Otis, a man who was once a stranger in Tikko's life, would morph into the intercessor working to bring us back together. But I fought back hard, I fought all the way. After the first beating I wanted to prove a point, demonstrate to Tikko his abuse would not be tolerated. I filed a restraining order. Otis though, would be the voice of reason. He would fight for me and abhor Tikko's behavior. He was taking on his role as father, for Tikko and for me.

"That girl was lost when you met her Tikko . . ." he would preach adamantly. "She's a good girl and she's going places. She's lied, made some terrible choices, but it ain't yo' job to punish her. You can't be hittin' on that girl."

Otis told it like it was. I couldn't lie to him. He was completely opposite of mother. He had been around the block more than once and he knew every trick the devil could muster up. He didn't profess to be a Christian but he believed in God—enough so to give him praise before every meal. He was married (balancing a love circus of his own), cursed about every fourth word, wore his hair in a ponytail and took pride in raising two very smart girls. He was interesting to say the least, but he was real.

Once our relationship started resembling that of Sterling and Shiloh's, Otis insisted it was time for Tikko and I to set out on our own. We became wanderers, we were homeless. We stayed in the same place for three nights at most. Our residences were many and with whomever would take us—family, friends and cheap $40 per night motels. To the indigent motel dwellers I was a piece of meat, I looked out of place, scared, slightly offended and they knew it, they smelled it. My fear attracted everything from lesbian hookers to assertive pimps. Every night the walk to our rat-infested room felt like the last march, a long cold journey down the dark corridor of death row; with the last stop being execution. Cowering behind his sturdy and protective frame, I would cling so tightly to Tikko's left forearm my fingernails would cause his skin to bleed. This was hell.

While our fights continued, the tone and topics changed. They were less severe—fewer blows to the head, but Tikko's anger still raged from the apparent frustration of a life going nowhere. Instead we were fighting about where to sleep and who to call next; where money would come from and how the two of us were going to eat on six dollars and twenty-five cents.

During the day while I worked, Tikko would hustle for money . . . and fuel. Roving from place to place meant exhausting a lot of resources. Gasoline prices were high and my raggedy old truck was always breaking down. It was as a 1993 Dodge Ram. It sat up high like a monster truck straight out of *Dukes of Hazard*; the rumble of its engine could be heard over a mile away. In the winter the truck cab was extremely cold, so much so we rode with blankets to keep us warm. In the hot days of summer the radiator ran hot. The smell of warming fluids and burning hoses was a sign it was time to stop. On those occasions Tikko had the process down packed. He'd pull the hissing truck into Otis' front driveway, pass the front door and head straight for the garden hose on the side of the house. I wasn't quite sure what he was doing under there, but felt a sense of relief when the temperature gauge slowly moved from hot to cold.

Tikko was crafty. He was good with his hands and he knew how to take care of us. When my mind would wander, thinking how we were in a good place, the devil would jerk me back almost to the point of getting whiplash; he reminded me daily what Tikko had done. He was still the man who beat me.

Truth be told, the abuse never stopped. It was as though Tikko became empowered by his ability to intimidate me, raising his voice in hysterical accusation when he thought I was cheating or making plans to leave him. I wasn't sure I wanted to leave. Our toxic relationship mix of love, survival and abuse undoubtedly was unhealthy, but it was normal, it was my normal. Leaving meant finding my way on my own—creating my own village with new friends and an uncertain future.

I wasn't ready to venture out. I was convinced, Tikko hurt; therefore unknowingly, he hurt me. The thought of me leaving him hurt him to the core. His broken and abusive past prevented him from learning how to cope with hurt and disappointment, so I would do whatever it took to protect him, including becoming the bull's-eye—the target of his pain.

Some nights were better than others. We were a passionate couple who loved to eat, kiss, laugh and do things normal couples do. We watched movies, played cards, and poked fun of the many walks of life that strolled in and out of our cheap motel we called home. Like Sterling and Shiloh, when we were good—we were good.

Although I was never really sexual, nor actually cared for sex in the way it was glorified on television and by friends like Sterling and Shiloh, Tikko was quite experienced and soon taught me things mother wouldn't have dared to discuss.

Tikko's world immersed him in a culture and around people who frequented strip clubs, consumed pornography daily and demanded sexual indulgence incessantly. Now, Tikko's world was my world. My mind and senses became submerged in filth and idolatry. Constant exposure to sex, drugs, abuse and neglect destroyed my ability to rationalize and to emotionally connect with people, both men and women. My virtue as a woman and as God's beloved daughter had been reduced to nothing, and in most cases, I was a willing participant.

Conceivably, my loss of personal and emotional connection with people left long before I met Tikko. Perhaps it occurred the first time I abandoned my children in search of self-pleasure, or when I extended my heart to my father in the form of a letter only for it to return void and full of rejection. Maybe I could blame the first person who robbed me of my innocence and my purity Sunday after Sunday in my small unsuspecting church home. Whoever was to blame, I was a walking, complying zombie; observing, participating, endorsing and existing in a world foreign to anything I had ever known. Emotionally, physically and spiritually, I was a dead woman walking.

Unlike the 'good days' clouded by a fog of fantasy and lewd living, other moments translated into nights of testing and pure torment. On many occasions I watched in horror as the man I loved literally "clicked" in front of me. It seemed as though he was possessed—something snapped; during his fits of rage he was an entirely differently person. Pupils enlarged with hate and body postured like a lion ready to pounce atop its prey, I shuttered at the stranger before me. Terrified I forced my eyes and head toward the floor—counting tiles, finding patterns in the carpet, I busied my eyes with whatever I could to ensure they didn't make contact with his.

Silently I would repeat, "If I'm quiet he'll just walk away." Or I would recite the one verse I knew would give me peace,

> [6] *Be strong and courageous. Do not be afraid or terrified because of them, for the Lord your God goes with you; he will never leave you nor forsake you. (Deuteronomy 31:6)*

> . . . I clung to that last part especially—*He would never leave nor forsake me.*

I prayed for God to save me. I prayed those nights Tikko would bang on the door with his fist, kicking and screaming he would kill me if I didn't come out. I prayed that time he shoved me into the closet, smacking me with his palms and with bags and anything else he could get his hands on; and I prayed when he seemed to protect me less and less—when I was left behind in our motel room of a home and at random people's houses when he had to go 'take care of business.'

I never stopped praying, but I felt God wasn't listening. I was a sinner begging the Savior's mercy. I was in too deep and was too ashamed to abandon my current existence, the people and the environment I had come to crave. No, I wanted a temporary fix; I wanted to be rescued not restored.

Eventually our cheating tricks and skillful thievery caught up with us. The owners of the street-side motel had finally connected the dots—we'd been paying our weekly rent with their credit card number. They were calling the police so literally, we ran. As fast as we could we grabbed our clothes encased within three rubber bins functioning as dresser drawers and sprinted for the truck—"Please Lord let this piece of junk start . . ." I threw up toward the sky in a thoughtless prayer. As we sped off, the police pulled up. We escaped another close encounter with The Law.

We had not been so lucky in times past. About this time, the protection order restricting me from the children had been reduced—permitting just one 2-hour visit with the children each weekend. The weekends were my time; I was transitioning back as mother. I survived Monday through Friday knowing the visit was soon forthcoming. Since Tikko and I were a packaged duo, we always made the trip together. I knew this made mother furious; the moment we arrived she retreated to her room and stayed there until I hollered up, "Mother, we're leaving now . . ."

Following one of our many trips across the state line to Kansas, we realized the gas tank was dangerously low. We were stuck; not enough gas to turn around and go back to mothers and no cash in hand, we decided we had no choice. No checks, no credit cards, nothing. How would we ever make it back home (wherever home was)?

"We'll just have to borrow some . . ." I whispered. I knew it sounded as foolish to Tikko as it sounded in my head. But the tables had turned, I was Clyde and he was Bonnie. The theft was my idea.

"Maybe we start pumping, walk into the store like we're going to pay for it and then pretend like we suddenly realized we forgot our wallets. They've got to let us go then . . ."

I could see Tikko wasn't totally psyched about the plan. It was risky and we were no strangers to run-ins with local law enforcement. But what other options did we have? We were law-breakers, a domestically violent couple with very few friends. We had nowhere to go and no one to call. This was it, we were going for it.

I'm pretty sure you know how this particular story ended without me boring you with all the dramatic details. For grins, here's a quick synopsis:

> Girl and boy pull into a small gas station in Kansas with the intention of stealing gas. Together, girl and boy proceed to pump gas and execute theft as planned. Girl gets scared so boy and girl panic. Plans fall apart and boy and girl take off in the rickety good-for-nothing Dodge Ram. Boy and girl become so distracted with fear they forget how to get to the highway—

the highway out of Kansas. Unbeknownst to boy and girl, the local police station is nearby—two blocks away to be exact. Boy and girl get pulled over by Lenexa, Kansas police; the K-9 unit—yes, the K-9 unit. Girl nearly has her arms chewed off as she's placed in the K-9 vehicle by mistake. Girl and boy are arrested and spend the night in jail. The next day, girl and boy are released from jail. Boy's father Otis foots the bill.

Speechless aren't you?

Something about our last "Otis bailout" gave Tikko and I both great pause. Perhaps it was something about the two of us being imprisoned together; together our reckless manner rendered us powerless. We realized something had to change. We were both much better than this. I desperately wanted to become a mother again and had become so intoxicated with living a hoodlum life it was literally making me sick. The conditions for getting my children back were simple: demonstrate change and responsibility by maintaining a steady job and providing a safe and habitable home for me and the kids. I thank God my season of neglect took place nearly a decade ago. Today, such negligence would have received a much harsher penalty and a far more painful social stigma—a very public badge of disgrace.

Going together for our visits to the twins made us realize, we were parents— mom and dad. The more we visited the harder leaving became. When I left Lenexa I cried profusely. I wanted my babies to come home with me. But I didn't have a home. Motel rooms simply weren't suitable and shacking up with friends was not an option, so together we sought after our new home.

For months we toiled. We worked hard at our respective jobs, applied for Section 8 housing and even secured a stable and honest source for sustenance; we were proud to receive our monthly food stamps—a comforting fact that every day we would eat. Together we were building the fabric of what would become our family.

By the time the twins returned we were rooted in a quaint three bedroom bungalow in the inner city. The children were mine again and now we were a family of four. Somehow I ignored the reality of where we lived; the sounds of gun shots and gangster rap flowing up and down our busy street all throughout the night. But I wasn't afraid, I had Tikko and this was his neighborhood. He had a family of his own—him, me and two tiny lives he vowed to protect at all costs.

Despite our newly created nest on 44th and Montgall, we still found ourselves drifting—from true direction and perhaps a greater, more intentional purpose. Everything about are lives continued to lack meaning. I was hungry for something and Tikko seemed satisfied with nothing. As a mother I tried to relive and recreate those earlier moments I had lost with the twins. From tea parties and bubble baths to painting toenails and playing video games, I did everything I could to demonstrate how sorry I was. I needed my children to know I was eternally sorry.

Despite having a more stable environment, Tikko's involvement with the family faded more and more. Many were the nights he was gone for seven to eight hours, leaving at dusk and returning at dawn. Here I was trying to reconstitute the family we lost, the family we never knew, and he continued to search for ways to run from it.

But I was determined to persevere. I didn't understand his resistance, but I had to make this work. I couldn't lose my children again. I imagine he felt replaced; overshadowed by a mother's joy in reuniting with the only true loves she'd ever known. I did my best to balance my love for babies and boyfriend both, but I needed him to understand. I hoped he would be patient yet compelled to join in the journey with me. I was determined to excel—with and for the children; it was time to go to greater heights. But Tikko stopped and watched. He was confused and must have felt neglected. Every night he pursued a secret life in the streets. My addiction however, was gone. My babies were my new drug of choice.

The year 2004 proved to be a time of testing and turning points. It would be a series of what I now believe were divine intercessions that would initiate my journey toward restoration. I was at the midway point along my continuum. Having learned I was pregnant again, I realized my life was still spinning—moving without purpose or precision. Shortly before our third child Erika was born, I secured a job as a senior administrative assistant with the Kansas

City Urban League. It was a miracle of an opportunity—working alongside prominent men and women of color with a prestigious and very important mission. It was here I met Gwendolyn Grant, president and CEO of the organization.

Ms. Grant was a savvy, overtly organized business woman whose dress was as sharp as her mind. A leader within the African American and Latino communities both local and national, she was a trailblazer to say the least. With Ms. Grant at the head, the Urban League's mission was to create opportunities and foster equality for minorities in all aspects of life—civic, cultural, social, economic and educational. Ms. Grant led by example and as Tikko would say, "She didn't take no mess."

Truthfully, I was terrified of Ms. Grant. Everything about her was exact, planned in advance, well communicated and preposterously clean; she hated clutter and wasn't afraid to call out clear offenders. I was one of them. Eight months pregnant, every day I woke up with just enough energy to slide on some slacks the size of circus tents and slick down my tangled hair weave that was two months overdue for a touch-up. I was a mess. I was tired, struggling daily to improve my role as mother for two very busy twins, and was still wrestling with the unpredictable temper of an uncompromising husband. Undoubtedly, the wear and tear of each new day was apparent. Ms. Grant could see it on my face, in my tardiness and clearly, in my dress.

I hated dressing up, particularly in business attire. I was sloppy and I knew it; wrinkled, short pants, scuffed shoes, it didn't matter. They were lucky I even made it to work. I know now, my outer demonstration was not a result of not knowing how to improve, but resulted from of a strong lack of care and frankly not wanting to. I was confident in my mind, "aint' nobody gonna change me . . ." hence the reason I was going nowhere.

My experience at the Urban League revealed much more than the importance of being on time and putting my best (and polished) satin leather pump forward. It became a season of self-reflection and self-awareness—I was messy, I was talented and had a few good ideas, but I was cutting myself short. I was ignoring my Godly calling and a slew of spiritual gifts in which I was designed to operate. The job was one of the most challenging experiences of my life. It was rough and it uncovered some of my greatest weaknesses.

It would be an earlier conversation with Ms. Grant followed by on one quiet Friday evening when I found myself gazing at the many plaques on her office wall, I realized her gifts were not just given, but had been earned—diligently worked for. Schooling was a major factor within this equation. She was a graduate of Park University, a prestigious university no doubt if it had produced the likes of Gwendolyn Grant. I had only completed two years of undergraduate school—plans derailed by an unexpected pregnancy and a couple of years of wandering in the wilderness of unruly living.

When my temporary position at the Urban League expired, it was clear I wasn't ready for the professional world. It was time to do better. I would go back to school, reclaim my purpose, and build a future my family and my God could be proud of.

When Erika was born I was well on my way toward refocusing. This time Tikko appeared to be on board—providing support and eliminating roadblocks along the way. By day I would work odd jobs, administrative gigs, sneaking in schoolwork and study time during lunch. At night after the kids were fed and bathed it was off to school to the Parkville campus more than thirty-five miles away. This was our routine every fall, spring, summer and winter—father bundling up three babies to make the forty-minute drive to retrieve the exhausted but determined mother from school, most times well after 10:30 at night.

As we pushed forward, our drive had shifted gears. Still, several questions remained; a greater purpose was still unclear. I couldn't shake the feeling something was missing. What were we doing? Where were we going? Tikko and I, although rowing simultaneously, clearly our oars were going in different directions. Where was our relationship going and where should it be headed? How could I expect God to continue opening doors and perform miracles in my life if I was failing to be obedient and sacrificial for Him?

And what about this God, the only God I believed in so faithfully as a child? I knew *of* God, but I didn't know Him personally. Who was God . . . now? I was bathed in a culture of all things Christian, all things holy and pure. But I had strayed so far from the Gospel I knew to be true. I had turned my back on God and his many expectations for my life. Boyfriend and God . . . I was ultimately uncommitted to both.

I wrestled with what would be the most important decisions of my life. Perhaps I should leave Tikko . . . I could make him leave. We were living in my house, on my Section 8 voucher, surviving with my income—couldn't I make him leave? But was that fair? We had struggled together, survived together—protected each other at the scariest of times; but what about those *other* times? At one time he was abusive, untrustworthy and seemed to be comfortable in his stagnant state. He was great with the children when he was calm and in most cases high on marijuana; but when reality and frustration settled in, he was frightening, loud and hurtful. I couldn't continue raising a family this way; this was not the type of environment that would produce healthy, contributing members of society.

Life at the Urban League—traveling in and around different social, professional and family circles—made me realize what a sound family life was supposed to be. My life wasn't normal, I longed to be normal. Searching for my normal meant returning to the one place I knew to be safe. It was a familiar place evoking memories around some sensational yet very trying times. I was going back to church—my home church in Kansas City, Kansas. Even then, what would be ten years later, the church where I had grown up was still the place, the sanctuary in which I knew I could find rest. Despite my altered and imprudent state, I knew two things to be true—God was real and He could not lie. If He said He would be there awaiting my return, I would believe God and seek His favor, I was ready to come back home.

> *Come to me, all you who are weary and burdened, and I will give you rest.*
>
> *(Matthew 11:28)*

Reflecting on this verse, I never knew if God meant for what seemed to be a very clear directive, to be taken literally or spiritually. Was He referring to those like me, who when eight months pregnant and saddled with two toddlers were literary exhausted every single day? Or, was He making this invitation to people like mother who were emotionally and physically worn—burdened with the load of loving a troubled child perhaps too much? I have to come realize now, Jesus is not in the business of sin and sorrow segregation. It makes no difference if the problem is figurative or literal, emotional or physical; He carries them all. Whatever our grief or crisis we bear, He has promised to provide relief if we just trust Him. Trust may not translate to an immediate reprieve from the problems at hand, but it does provide the undeniable assurance, He's got this; but before all of this, we must first surrender ourselves and the struggles we carry completely over to Him. While He is a supernatural God with supernatural powers, He is a God of free will. His love is not designed to choose surrender for us, but it is strong enough to hold us when we say, "Ok Lord, I've tried everything, I'm turning my life over to you."

I was at that point, ready to surrender. I had tried everything and had gotten nowhere. I knew I needed to be cleaned up, fixed up and glued together too. When the devil kept nudging time and time again, "You're too far gone; you've done too much to go back . . ." I remembered a verse Sister Gilbert once read in Sunday school,

> *If we confess our sins, he is faithful and just and will forgive us our*
> *sins and purify us from all unrighteousness. (1 John 1:9)*

I was convinced; I had nothing to lose.

Returning to church was an experience in itself. Most familiar faces had gone, the congregation had become significantly smaller in size, and with every Sunday service the devil concocted at least one hundred-and-one reasons why I should say 'forget it,' and not go. Coming back with three children in one hand and an old Bible soaked with my anxiety-filled sweat in the other, we were fearful of how we would be received. An unmarried couple, faces guilty with signs of fornication, fighting and relationship failure, we were sure those saints would run us right out the door. But they didn't; in fact, when we walked in they stopped, they looked, and clapped. Every Sunday following, we were one of them.

At Christ Temple we met the Davis'—Darryl and Lisa. Pastor Davis was a young, vibrant pastor from Washington, D.C.; a refreshing change to the many who preceded him. When he preached I would laugh as he pronounced words like "church" and "Lord;" his East coast accent was quite amusing, but compelled me to listen even more intently.

His wife Lisa was just as dynamic. A praise-filled woman of God, Sister Davis loved to worship. Hailing from St. Louis, Missouri, she was the daughter of a Bishop and had played the piano from the time she could reach the keys. Every Sunday when we arrived to church, the sanctuary would be filled with sounds of glorious gospel music; I couldn't help but enter with a heart and spirit ready for praise.

Together they were a power couple—in ministry, in their respective professions and in love. They radiated with adoration for each other and the respect shared between them as man and wife was nothing I had ever witnessed before.

"How could anyone possibly love someone that much?" I marveled, wondering if I would ever love Tikko in that way. But I yearned for that love, I wanted *their* love; a love that could only be found in the confines of a Godly marriage.

When we met the Davis' we were struggling to stay afloat. We were growing professionally and improving as parents, but our relationship status was still a pile of wreckage in need of sorting, salvaging and repair. But Darryl and Lisa took special interest in our affairs. They made countless visits to our home and even watched the kids when we needed time to just be still—just Tikko and me alone together. They quickly became much more than ministers and evolved into mentors and more importantly, role models for our shaky and at times volatile relationship.

With each encounter the Davis' were clear about what true love really looks like, what it does, what it doesn't do and what it tolerates, for better and for worse. Man to man, woman to woman, they implored us to consider our choices and our consequences; they explained a true relationship with each other and with Christ meant a romantic relationship based in holiness and purity.

Feeling pressured and perhaps confused, Tikko and I danced and danced around the possibility of marriage. I harbored hate and unforgiveness and was convinced a marriage rooted in pain and distrust would never take flight. He felt rushed and unready; the idea of committing his life to both God and woman was a frightening and intangible thought. Against our wills and our sense of readiness, we would take the plunge. The proposal was practically meaningless . . . I frankly don't remember it. What I do recall was in the form of an ultimatum. I wanted to keep pressing towards my goal of restoration with

Christ. He would marry me or leave, those were the options. We married in November 2005.

You know that expression "kids change everything?" Well for us, marriage so appropriately fit this same mantra. I'm not sure what it was exactly—perhaps it was the ring or the makeshift ceremony we had immediately following Sunday service; but whatever it was, it felt good. Things were solid—at least on the surface. Feeling one step closer to holiness, marriage seemed to empower and unequivocally enhance my outlook on our family's future. Tikko was my husband and I was his wife. The previous five years hadn't been for naught. If only for a brief moment, I felt validated, I was legitimate. If we could conqueror homelessness, scandal and abuse, we could conquer anything.

With my mind focused on living a purpose-driven life, I embraced a spirit of worship and praise like never before. Singing was my passion since the time I could speak, but now I was a woman with a testimony: the greatness of God was the inspiration behind my voice. My singing was driven by praise; my praise was an outcome of my troubled past; my past was framing the story of my life—a life being restored and reunited with Christ. And slowly my stories took the form of written songs. Each one represented a cycle of praise; I was in a good place.

As a wanderer—without Christ, I was selfish, absorbed in my own suffering and pain. But every day in my marriage and in my worship, I grew to find joy in serving God and others. Whenever possible, I would aid with youth events, Bible studies and worship services where before I would not have dared. Here I was, more than a decade later, ministering to children as Sister Gilbert had ministered to me. We would serve together—mother, Sister Gilbert and me—in the kitchen preparing meals for Vacation Bible School and during Sunday school teaching ages one through seventy-three. Even at times when I was physically exhausted and just didn't want to be bothered, I prayed for God to increase my patience, my love and my kindness toward everyone I served, especially toward my husband Tikko. While I hadn't amassed a total understanding of who God was, I knew He was real and He was at work in me. I knew enough to pray and to seek some form of presence in and with Him.

At Christ Temple I learned it's impossible to take risks without producing some very real and oftentimes unexpected revelations and requirements from

God. Although the Lord never asked me to fix myself before coming back to Him, He expected me to change—to abandon and to walk away from my former ways. He also expected me to be obedient, not only in words and in body movements, but in actions—tangible, concrete actions. Taking action toward Godly living would require me to take risks. I would have to face my frustrations, my hate and my unforgiving spirit, and obediently adopt the fruits of *His* Holy Spirit: love, joy, peace, patience, kindness, goodness, faithfulness, gentleness and self-control. He wanted my sacrifice, wholly and faithfully. I would take a risk, trust Him with my life and walk blindly but confidently with my hand in His.

A proponent of walking in blind faith, Pastor Davis was astonishing. I was captivated by his willingness to take risks; he insisted on delivering God's message as it was endowed to him. I'm sure some may have felt his delivery was much too radicle, but I on the other hand thrived off the raw dose of Holy Word mixed with modern day humor, brashness and reality.

I remember one Sunday when he graced the pulpit following the last choir selection just as he had done every Sunday before. This particular Sunday he approached carrying a big box. It looked to be a gift box wrapped in shiny gold paper as those it was plucked from some unsuspecting family's Christmas tree. As he held the box for the congregation to see he began explaining its purpose. He described the awesome responsibility God had bestowed upon him as a minister, to ensure everyone within his reach was equipped with the Gospel— the *good news* that Jesus saves. He explained how it didn't matter who we were, what wrong we had done, or how grimy we thought our sins had made us. If we believed in Jesus Christ as the one true Savior who died and rose from death in order to redeem us from our sins, we were guaranteed eternal life in heaven with Christ. After this life, when our earthly life was over, we would live again and reign with our Lord, Jesus Christ forever. Wow.

The gift he held was not really a gift at all. As he turned the front face of the package around, there a small, but very important note read,

> *Open this box in case of rapture. If it is here and we are not, this means we, Christ's children, are gone. We have been taken to glory just as Jesus promised. Unfortunately if you are reading this note, you and perhaps many of our friends and loved ones that remain*

there with you, where not prepared; they weren't ready to come along. While we cannot predict what will happen from here, we only pray God's mercy will be with you until your life's end. We love you, we miss you. Your Christ Temple Family.

When he finished, the only sound heard was absolute silence. I glanced at Tikko, he didn't say a word. My thoughts moved quickly from him to a reflection of my own life. Where did I stand? What was my position? Would I be the one forced to open the gold box? I didn't want to be; I trembled at the thought of being left behind. I didn't want Jesus to come and leave without me. I wanted to meet Him and to thank Him. I wanted to kiss Him for holding and protecting my children every night I left them behind. From that day forward, I would follow Christ indefinitely. No turning back, I was persuaded—I wasn't turning back.

Go ye therefore, and teach all nations, baptizing them in the name of the Father, and of the Son, and of the Holy Ghost: Teaching them to observe all things whatsoever I have commanded you: and, lo, I am with you always, even unto the end of the world. Amen.
(Matthew 28:19-20)

Chapter 9
Mind, Body and Mission

Let me make one point very clear. I'd like to tell you that once I recommitted my focus and total devotion to Jesus Christ, everything miraculously improved from there—my life was nothing but butterflies and blue skies and my plethora of problems disappeared. Well, committing to Christ—be it your first, second or third time doesn't quite work that way. Yes it is true, ". . . if any man be in Christ, he is a new creature: old things are passed away; behold, all things are become new" (2 Corinthians 5:17). And yes, Christ confirmed . . . "In all things we are more than conquerors through Him who loved us." (Romans 8:37). But He also advised His children in love, "Be not deceived; God is not mocked: for whatsoever a man soweth, that shall he also reap." (Galatians 6:7).

I had sown an assortment of seeds, the blossoms of which greatly shamed my family, my professional reputation and God. I didn't think of God as a mean-spirited being who was in the business of teaching His children a lesson through pain and punishment, but I knew returning to His sanctuary would only be the beginning of my reunification with Him. It was not enough to feel repentant momentarily; to profess His name through songs and worship. Reunification would require remorse, self-examination, sacrificial living and downright change, particularly in the most uncomfortable of places—my marriage and my personal relationships.

Even though Tikko and I were attending church together, it was in the house of worship I felt we were the furthest apart. It was like we were on two totally different planets—me in the hemisphere of confession, contrition and complete surrender and He in the realm of *"How much longer do I have to be here?"* I knew He was only there because of me and the kids. He knew how much it meant to me to build a family with a foundation rooted in faith. I had started so wrong and had a lot to make up for. I was fashioning my family after those from my childhood village—the Mackays, the Careys, the ones with Christ at the center.

I'd be furious on Sunday mornings looking into the crowd while leading a rousing rendition of *Bless that Wonderful Name*. There he was, sitting amidst the other saints who were singing and dancing up on their feet. The sermon would follow soon thereafter; out of the church he quietly crept just as the pastor approached the podium.

"It's not your job to save Tikko . . ." mother would say. She reminded me of the days when he didn't come at all. "Remember when it was just you and the kids coming by yourselves? Praise God Tikko's coming to church at all—that in itself is a major change."

I nodded my head in annoyance and disregard. I couldn't understand why Tikko hadn't heeded God's call. Did he know who God was? Christ had spared our very lives. Did Tikko not realize how fortunate we were; that in our prolonged season of absolute defiance, God *could have* wiped us off the face of the earth? How could he hear the message of salvation, how freely God made eternal life available for everyone, and still—do nothing. Why wasn't he running to the Savior, pleading for forgiveness and for Jesus to take charge?

His resistance troubled me, it angered me actually. Soon I felt myself disregarding him totally. In my mind I couldn't take him seriously if making a decision between life and death wasn't a serious concern for him. Our relationship was changing and weakening. I wanted to grow in Christ, in family life and in my career. He was convinced I had drastically changed, revolted, transformed and turned against him. He didn't hate the new me, but he certainly didn't like her. He told me on many occasions He had been booted to second place—lagging behind on my priority list behind kids and Christian living. He didn't mind the church thing so much but the trips to the park, late night coursework online and the constant searching and applying for jobs made him irate. He was becoming increasingly bitter.

We argued every day, most times well into the night. Each time he danced around a fine line with his own self-appointed authority and irrepressible emotions, creeping right up to the border of anger and physical abuse. I could tell he wanted to hit me, but instead he screamed louder and with a heart-stopping rage. I wasn't sure what was stopping him but I antagonized, I pushed him further; I welcomed the contact so it wouldn't come as a total surprise. My arrogance had proliferated to unflinching. I was done with my feminine victimization. If he wanted a fight, a crazed, bitter woman with nothing to lose was what he was sure to get. My intolerance of his rantings only seemed to fuel his fury. I knew he struggled with finding words, a sense of communication normalcy in which to express his fears and frustrations. I knew the tactics to which he resorted were the only things he knew, but I was determined to exploit his weaknesses just as he had exposed mine. I recognized his limitations and his inner stumbling blocks, his and mine. In my determination to act as sentence executioner, I became hypocritical within my own marriage and in my heart where Christ supposedly lived. I didn't love, my patience was obsolete; I was certainly not ready to forgive.

Although my marriage was still a rocky road, I felt life in being restored. Fully denying the devil's claims that my previous sins would prevent me from profiting from the many blessings I was due as an heir of Jesus Christ, I took risks and waited to see how forgiveness and faith would materialize. I threw up prayers, hopes and claimed expectations, watching eagerly to see how God would respond. I knew His role was far from that of a genie to be beseeched with lofty dreams and desires, so I prayed for Him not to perform miracles, but simply to intervene. I was surrendering completely to Him. I was ready to walk totally in His will for my life—whatever it should entail; I was ready to experience God. I had experienced "reglionship," going through the motions, mimicking the ideal Christian lifestyle. Now I longed for relationship.

After leaving the Urban League, I was determined to hone my skills and discover my brand—who I was, what I stood for, and the platform I had to offer everyone around me in hopes of changing the world. I had big dreams and served an even bigger God. I knew I was in over my head with jobs and relationships in times past, but I knew with God going before me, He would open doors and reveal opportunities beyond my exceptionally limited and carnal imagination.

At this point along my continuum I found myself in an exciting but very uncertain place. This place was an area filled with thick grey matter. Not as thick and entrapping as quicksand, but a grey matter that toys with your emotions, shifting your outlook from positively hopeful one minute to scared and apprehensive the next.

New jobs, new skills in public relations and emergency management, coupled with two new degrees made me feel my life and my career were finally out of the harbor. I was sailing on open seas. But other days I was filled with trepidation. Balancing work and family was a daunting task and the one person who believed he suffered the most was overtly bitter and particularly expressive about my newfound journey. Tikko was convinced his wife had left him behind.

Despite my balancing act being far from mastered, I continued to take leaps. This time it was for a management-level position with the local city government. It was a long shot, but God had ordained the opportunity before the position was even posted. It would be a life-altering experience—professionally, spiritually and physically. It was here I found myself edging toward the peak of my turning points. When I landed the job, I was surprised beyond belief. Here I was twenty-seven, no management experience and way outside of my league when it came to talking fiscal budgets and capital improvement projects with senior leadership staff during the weekly roundtable.

It would be the city's administrators, Eric Johnson and Todd Pelham who would take a chance on the rehabilitated scallywag who hadn't held a real job for more than two years. I realize now they must have known, or at least had an inkling of the chaos and instability that lie behind my tired eyes and a few, but significant missteps. Even still, they remained faithful to fashioning me into a smart and virtuous leader. The move was risky but their commitment, their Godly kindness, would soon materialize; elevating their protégé, the City's good name and the strength of their organization to a national stage. One instance in particular would forever change the way I viewed these two men, both as professionals and as Christians.

Even though I had secured an impressive job with a more than generous salary, our family was still struggling to make ends meet. Tikko's work was irregular and I had explored multiple avenues in which to generate extra income; yes, even selling Mary Kay. Unfortunately nothing seemed to stick and frustration was a persistent guest at every meal. Frustration soon turned to desperation and without delay, the devil was ready and attentive, actively reminding me of the mischievous roots from which I had recently broken away. He brought to memory the many credit cards I had stolen, the checks I forged and the other schemes I used to make sure children and family were fed. But I couldn't do that, I remembered the shiny gold box. I was confident God wanted more for me and no earthly gain was worth me being left behind.

Confidence however, can never supplant the concrete security found in the Word of God. Before, I was rooted in the world, finding pleasure in my own selfish desires and shallow wisdom. In order to be truly recommitted to Christ I would have to become reestablished and re-rooted in God's word. His Word would ensure my stability in a viable foundation for life, one which would enable me to resist the devil and his many tricks and ridiculous lies. Unfortunately, while my commitment was stable, my adherence to the Word was not. So when the devil came a temptin', I panicked. My biblical instability gave way to sin.

As the Communications Manager for the city, my job was to keep residents informed. Produced from my office were a number of publications, including a weekly electronic newsletter and a quarterly magazine. With the dawn of real-time information sharing, product promotion and social media, the e-news concept was pretty straight forward. People desire to be in the know; sometimes they became information recipients without even asking. E-mails were a quick and easy way to get good information, keep the stuff you want and spam the stuff you don't. This was my rationale. In addition to city updates, I was convinced I had good information to share. I would send the 6,500 recipients of the City's newsletters my personal business advisory:

> *For all your Mary Kay products and personal needs, call Merideth Parrish today.*

I know what you're thinking . . . *How stupid could she be? Who could one do such a senseless thing?* Would you believe me if I said I didn't know any better? Truthfully, I don't think I did. I had become so convinced by the seductive nature of my torn inner man and the irrational possibility that my novel business venture would actually produce a favorable response that I fell into the pit of my own lies. I was so deeply fixed in a problem-saturated coma that

I couldn't look past finding an immediate resolution; any future consequences were far beyond my current state of mind.

When word came back to Eric and Todd, I knew I was done; a freak decision and a moment of panic would destroy all hopes for a productive and prosperous future. When it became decision time, I had three choices: confess, run or lie. However, I had recommitted to Christ and mistakes were just going to be a part of the transition. There was no way around it, either I would serve the Lord—unashamed and fully transparent of my many flaws and weaknesses, or I would continue living a life of shame and aimless wandering. I chose to stand, confess what I had done and trust God to take me through the events to follow. Maturity would be found in my capacity to not only learn from my mistakes, but also in my choice to trust God to carry me through the consequences, not to bail me out of them.

As I walked slowly to Eric's office for a meeting called the following Friday night, I prepared for the fateful words I was sure would come, "Merideth, clean out your office . . ."

Instead he rebuked my actions, counseled as to why this behavior is highly inappropriate in a position of public service, paused slightly and said,

". . . and frankly Merideth, the only reason we're not letting you go is because you were honest, you made a very stupid and irresponsible mistake, but you were honest . . ."

It took every fiber in my body to remain composed despite the quivering pulse in my stomach and the swell of tears just at the edge of spillover behind my weakening eyelids. I couldn't believe it; the truth had set me free. As disbelieving as I was, the truth had actually set me free. In that moment God was revealed in real, human form. Jesus Christ had interceded (through Eric and Todd), going before God the Father to appeal for my pardon. It wasn't necessary and it certainly was underserved. So this is what it meant to be saved. *This* was God.

Being forgiven gave me a great sense of empowerment and importance. I was a person of value, not only to God my Father, but to the managers He had sent to mentor and counsel me. I was honored Eric and Todd chose to salvage me and my career. In all my years of feeling insignificant and unloved, God demonstrated in yet another occasion, this was certainly not the case.

Feeling empowered helped me to remain focused. The financial problems persisted, but I pressed on. My weekly worries were transformed into prayers for daily sustainment. If God promised to care for the birds of the air which are incapable of worry and do not store provisions beyond the needs of the day, surely He would supply the needs of His children. Soon my new roots were growing and were beginning to anchor; I was learning to trust God completely, He and his word.

> [25] *"Therefore I tell you, do not worry about your life, what you will eat or drink; or about your body, what you will wear. Is not life more than food, and the body more than* clothes? [26] *Look at the birds of the air; they do not sow or reap or store away in barns, and yet your heavenly Father feeds them. Are you not much more valuable than they?*
>
> [33] *But seek first his kingdom and his righteousness, and all these things will be given to you as well.* [34] *Therefore do not worry about tomorrow, for tomorrow will worry about itself. Each day has enough trouble of its own." (Matthew 6:25-26, 33-34)*

Not a year into my position with the City, I found myself coordinating one of the biggest events of the City's history, a first for the entire Kansas City metropolitan area. The popular reality TV talent series *American Idol* was coming to Blue Springs, Missouri: a celebratory homecoming complete with radio stops, a parade and a special concert for the show's Season 7 semi-finalist (and would be season winner) David Cook. With less than a week to prepare, the producers of the nationally-televised reality show provided little direction or restriction; a few do's and don'ts, but otherwise, it was our duty to make Blue Springs and David shine. Now more than five years later, the week's events are nothing more than a distant memory. Needless to say the public spectacle was a spectacle no doubt, but was executed to nearly perfection—tens of thousands of screaming fans, hours of community gridlock, national media coordination and all. It was David's moment, but my God's victory. To this day I don't know how we pulled that thing off, but each time I recall it I nod my head and laugh, never remiss in giving God the glory.

Having given birth to our fourth child Ethan, Tikko and I were in parenting mode full-throttle. Everything about our lives was busy. After the *American Idol* whirlwind, we were full-time parents of four, working professionals and part-time scout parents, living in the small rural community of Grain Valley, Missouri just four miles east of the now noteworthy city of Blue Springs.

Balancing life in a new home, with a new baby and a newfound love for work and success was exciting, unpredictably so. Together Tikko and I felt we had arrived; we were finally gaining momentum and even attempting to temper the many selfish scuffles we so regularly exchanged. We were loving life, embracing opportunities, spirits were high . . . so was my weight.

It was during this time of change and growth that I saw a picture of myself. Everything about me had expanded—mind, mission *and body*. Busyness had translated into countless uncontrollable sessions of snacking, fast-food and binge eating. Butterfingers and Double-Stuffed Oreos had become the perfect companions to stress and financial worry. There was something about the way the cream-filled cookie opened so delicately within my eager hands, unveiling a white patty of sugary, sweet bliss. My eyes would close, images of celestial satisfaction dancing from tongue to brain as the thick decadent cream made contact with the roof of my mouth. I was having a love affair with food. I weighed 258 pounds.

Again, God had an app for that. At the time, Blue Springs volunteers were spearheading a grassroots effort—Blue Springs F.I.T. *(Families In Training)* to promote family fitness and the maintenance of good health. Eager to support anything involving the city I had grown to love, I became an active member of everything F.I.T.

I was soon inspired by one of the initiative's co-chairs and CEO of the local medical center, Annette Small. During a kick-off event for Blue Springs F.I.T, Annette shared her story. She had lost over 100 pounds as a result of joining Weight Watchers. I was amazed. Her success sounded like such a wildly unattainable goal, but I was determined just as I had been in so many other instances when defeat seemed unavoidable, to pursue the impossible. I asked God and Annette to walk me through the process.

At that event I committed publically, in front of hundreds of strangers and colleagues, to lose 50 pounds within the next twelve months. If successful I would mostly likely break the 200-pound mark; I hadn't seen the 100's since before Erika was born. With that very public pledge, the race was on. I joined *Weight Watchers Online* and tracked every morsel that entered my mouth. I became consumed with the idea of not consuming. I focused on becoming a woman who ate to live, not one who lived to eat. I surrounded myself with fellow Weight Watchers members, which seemed to be conveniently sprinkled everywhere I went—church, school, work, you name it, those "WOWW" women as I call them (Women on Weight Watchers) were everywhere.

Controlled eating coupled with a disciplined workout schedule proved to be invaluable. Although I seemed to lose weight almost immediately, the pursuit of better health wasn't always a walk in the park. It was more like eating cake without flour, sugar or icing. It was rough and at times I was bitter. Diminishing my addiction to food felt as though my right and left arms had been cut off . . . with a butter knife. Many nights I was convinced I couldn't cope, I should just give in; I wasn't going to make it one more day. But it became those times when God's grace proved more than sufficient; just calling His name would get me through. Sometimes I prayed, and occasionally I ran for miles until I couldn't run anymore. Most nights I wrote songs until my fingers were cramped and sore—all to avoid fornicating with food. Within twelve months, a new me had emerged. I had lost more than twice my goal. By late 2010 I was 100 pounds lighter; I was a *Brand New Funkier Me* (This became the name of a self-empowering song I wrote and with pride published on iTunes. Needless to say it earned a chart-topping $3.50; but it didn't matter, it was my song, the victorious anthem of a new woman with a new body and a new appreciation for life).

The new me gave way to new hope and even greater expectations, both for the future and for myself. The next year following the *Great Shred* proved to be a time of great harvest. I was hired for a prime position with a prominent federal agency, my job would be to develop plans, create communication strategies and assist in delivering disaster information. At the same time, the makers of *Weight Watchers Online* would call me personally, inviting me to share my story and my weight loss success with the world through a national TV campaign. Was I dreaming? This couldn't be my life. Almost on cue the devil brought to memory the many lies I told, the people I once cheated and the innocent loved ones I had so willfully betrayed. I rebuked him and his venomous thoughts immediately. For the moment, I knew who I was and to whom I belonged. I recanted with the promises my Father had endowed unto me,

[1] If you fully obey the Lord your God and carefully follow all his commands I give you today, the Lord your God will set you high above all the nations on earth. [2] All these blessings will come on you and accompany you if you obey the Lord your God:

[3] You will be blessed in the city and blessed in the country.

[4] The fruit of your womb will be blessed, and the crops of your land and the young of your livestock—the calves of your herds and the lambs of your flocks.

[5] Your basket and your kneading trough will be blessed.

[6] You will be blessed when you come in and blessed when you go out.

[7] The Lord will grant that the enemies who rise up against you will be defeated before you. They will come at you from one direction but flee from you in seven.

[8] The Lord will send a blessing on your barns and on everything you put your hand to. The Lord your God will bless you in the land he is giving you.

[9] The Lord will establish you as his holy people, as he promised you on oath, if you keep the commands of the Lord your God and walk in obedience to him. [10] Then all the peoples on earth will see that you are called by the name of the Lord, and they will fear you. [11] The Lord will grant you abundant prosperity—in the fruit of your womb, the young of your livestock and the crops of your ground— in the land he swore to your ancestors to give you.

[12] The Lord will open the heavens, the storehouse of his bounty, to send rain on your land in season and to bless all the work of your

hands. You will lend to many nations but will borrow from none. [13] *The Lord will make you the head, not the tail. If you pay attention to the commands of the Lord your God that I give you this day and carefully follow them, you will always be at the top, never at the bottom.* [14] *Do not turn aside from any of the commands I give you today, to the right or to the left, following other gods and serving them. (Deuteronomy 28:1-14)*

Convinced my seasons of testing had subsided, I grew settled, almost complacent in beseeching the full nature and consistent presence of God. We had established roots in a new church home, but failed to keep Jesus as the ever present guest behind our private bedroom walls. Sure we prayed at nights, before meals and when finance companies threatened to repossess. But as a family unit, we neglected to embody the traits of Christ's church, His earthly body. I couldn't shake the feeling we were still so far from the Word and the will of God.

Like clockwork, I felt a deep yearning, similar to the sensation I had felt so many times prior. Progress was good and success was gratifying, but in my heart I was sure there had to be more. What was God's purpose for my life, what was my true and intended calling? To be a mother, a singer, an employee, a wife, a leader . . . I ached for a greater mission I could call my own.

Chapter 10
Me, Him, Them Revealed

Transitioning to a new job is never easy. In most cases it's a hybrid of chaos and anticipation. The uncertainty that exists around the change in atmosphere, the work you'll be doing and the people you'll be doing it with, is enough to drive you crazy if you let it. Me, I wasn't stressed. I figured I had been through so much already and was overtly transparent about my many flaws and shortfalls. While you never really can come out and say during the final job interview, "By the way, I'm a reformed criminal, now born-again Christian . . ." I revealed absolutely everything I could remember during an extensive background check. In my mind it was a miracle I had made it this far.

If there was one thing I wasn't prepared for, it was the great scrutiny and personal discretion my new position would require. Prior to leaving the city, the local newspaper featured a story around my departure and the great enthusiasm in which I looked forward to charting new waters. Imagine my surprise when I received an email from the person who would be my new boss which basically said, ". . . the article, highly inappropriate, the representation of my new role . . . misconstrued, almost arrogant in form. And by the way, welcome to our office."

The email was only a precursor of the challenges and at times sheer torment that was to follow. When I joined the already closely knit team I asked questions, probed in confusion and made suggestions (sometimes in ignorance). I was trying to learn the ropes yet assert the value I knew I could offer. I felt like a nagging child just trying to be heard.

After only one year, I was sure I had made a mistake. As much as I tried, I just couldn't fit in. Being a social bug had never been a problem in jobs or situations past, but here in this new role—a strange and unfamiliar environment—I was intentionally left out of emails, after-work invitations and weekend gatherings at the boss' house. I wasn't a member of their team, more like the water boy tagging along for the ride. This was a strange but somewhat reminiscent memory. I hadn't felt so rejected since my exile from the third grade playground more than twenty years ago. I missed my Blue Springs family; they were my safety net amidst my many accepted flaws.

It wasn't long before I realized I was a woman in mixed company. As much as I could tell, I was the only professed Christian on my team. I didn't swear, I didn't drink and outside of work, I had nothing of common value to share. Was this my mission? I hoped not, I wasn't ready. Certainly not ashamed of my faith and my Christian character, I wasn't sure if I could handle a bipartisan battle between worldliness and faith. I was Job and the devil was taunting, "Lord, try Merideth, certainly she will deny you and crumble under pressure . . ." It was me versus the devil himself and I was clearly outnumbered.

A major event that spring would disrupt our normal operations. Our entire team would be dispatched into the field for months to aid individuals whose lives were devastated by disaster. Each of us was given a very specific role. Soon, the entire team made its way to the heart of the devastation, everyone but me. I had a different function, working in a location more than four hours away from the rest of my team. But I welcomed the challenge, embracing the opportunity to learn a new and unfamiliar role. The exposure gave way to an entirely new range of learning. I thrived in the shadows of seasoned colleagues and mentors who provided the guidance and professional molding I so desperately needed a year ago.

When conditions stabilized, my team who was once working down range returned to their home office, everyone but me. I would stay in the field for two more months, a lifetime for a wife and mother of four kids who was unsure of her purpose and the value if any, of the work she did day after day. By far, my time in the field (four months in total), was the most sobering experience of my life. I had never felt so far from home, from comfort and from love. I felt abandoned, and deliberately so. The only message I received from my boss of one year—he was leaving the agency to pursue greener pastures. No boss, no direction, no clue what I was going to do. I couldn't understand why God had brought me to such a divine and ideal opportunity to let me suffer and then leave me behind.

For one hundred and twenty nights I sought understanding from the Lord. Why was I still here? What point was this proving? I wrestled with my heart, mind and emotional stamina. In my restlessness and spiritual impatience I became increasingly convinced it was time to move on. I scoured job boards and position announcements. Out of three hundred twenty-two resume submissions, not one response came; not an email, not a letter, not a phone call. What in the world was going on? "Why this place Lord, why so long, where are you?" I demanded.

"I can't take this anymore . . . I feel so lost . . . How is this good for the kids?" I would cry to mother.

"Just trust God, hold on to His word. He knows the plans He has for you and your future," she assured.

"His plans are holy . . . they're working for your good. If you trust Him, He'll take you through this storm" she would affirm unwaveringly.

I didn't understand, but I believed her just the same. I discontinued my job search, replaced worry with prayer and my fear with fasting. I put my nose to the ground and pressed on.

As the weeks grew in number, my period of isolation became a season of hope and praise. When my faith was floundering God revealed His grace in a capacity beyond anything I'd ever known. Truth be told, God's grace and His deep enduring love had never changed. This was the same God and the same grace that had covered my life for the last thirty years:—in the Jeep, in the apartment, in the shadows of an abusive relationship, and now in an unsure and uncomfortable place. He had kept me all this time according to His promise and His divine will. All I needed to do was walk through the experience, observing in amazement as He empowered me with a renewed and supernatural strength. This was God, my supernatural hero.

Soon, God provided great clarity through the faithfulness and comfort of family and close friends. In my path He would place new supports—Andrea, Dianne, Crystal and Cindy. As wise women they counseled and encouraged, helping me to navigate through the ropes of a real and sometimes ugly life. Through these women I came to understand the significance of our work. We were servants playing a small but important part in a far greater ministry; one that reached well beyond our office walls.

They taught me how to embrace the ideas of others more than my own, to value people above work achievements and to pursue solutions instead of proliferating problems. When challenges arise, they cautioned "choose your company carefully, seek counsel from Christ-followers and know that prayer is good, but the Bible keeps answers to every occasion known to man."

The four matriarchs became my women of faith, the network through which I discovered the true meanings of sacrifice, service and trust. Everything about them was compellingly captivating and filled with the divine spirit of God. As I modeled my patience and demeanor after theirs, I began looking internally to determine what value I too could offer this mighty unit of faith. I did all I could to focus less on myself, deliberately positioning my mind, heart and feet around serving the needs of others. I thought back to the events that had become my life and realized just how much God's grace and loving kindness had delivered me. I wasn't free of burdens and struggles, and even now worried that God wasn't exactly listening. But it became undoubtedly clear, I had a story to share, a message telling others to hold on to their faith. God is still faithful and has always been. Even if we've strayed or feel He's so far away, He is ever present and exercising His perfect will for our lives and for the world around us.

From my field location in Columbia, thoughts of God's mercy spilled over into countless songs of praise. I wrote without limitation, capturing everything I could remember—the feelings of doubt and isolation, periods of abuse and my ongoing journey toward Godly restoration. I immersed myself in the Word and embedded my ears in the teachings of those who delivered it well. Instead of mindless music accompanying my morning commute, I embraced the ministries of John MacArthur and Joyce Meyer, and added a new repertoire of musicians to my playlist; psalmists like Mandisa, Chris Tomlin, Newsboys and Natalie Grant. There was something about the words each artist transformed into music. They told stories, helped hurting hearts and revealed the most important truths one would ever hear. Contemporary Christian music was an unfamiliar genre, nothing I had heard before. But I loved this music. I was captivated from the first introduction; everything about it—the words, the delivery and the melodies themselves were so rich, so deep and so pure. It was worship that reflected the very nature of my heart—a simple but surreal spirit of praise.

I felt purpose emerging, a testimony being refined. Through my worship I continued to write songs depicting my life's story. Songs like *Reclaimed, It's Only a Test,* and *When My Soul Cries Out*, were fashioned out of miracles, each one representing a different point along my continuum. This time though, I wasn't writing to be discovered or to be signed to a major record label. I was writing my love songs to God.

Spring blossoms had closed and maple trees were turning by the time my field assignment was complete. I headed home not realizing my work and my life's true mission was just taking flight.

At home in my absence, Tikko was mom, dad, babysitter, seamstress and tutor. His role as the stay-at-home dad was something we had agreed to when it was apparent this latest career change would significantly disrupt our home life as we knew it. On the outside it appeared Tikko had grown increasingly comfortable in his domestic disposition. Little did I know, in his mind the position was more enfeebling than empowering; almost daily he was forced to defend the masculinity of his responsibilities despite their resemblance of very typical matriarch roles.

Each stint away from home produced heightened conversations and anxiety-filled resistance. For me, it was a season of uncertainty, a mental and emotional challenge each time I headed back to battle. For Tikko it produced moments of insecurity and apprehension. While he was at home he was left to wonder if anything or better yet anyone else had captured my attention. With every assignment as I hurried to complete some last-minute packing, he prodded with concern, "How long will you be there, where are you going? . . ." his wandering mind no doubt had left him sleepless the night before. I contested and reassured, "You know this is what we signed up for. I have a job to do babe . . . I'm not sure how long I'll be gone."

I couldn't wait to leave, his questions were irritating and they made me resent him all the more. He was making my departure even more difficult to handle.

I just needed him to support me, help me pack and stand at the edge of the driveway—he and the kids waving goodbye. I needed him to be the Hollywood husband (or wife, I'll let you be the critic), confident his partner was doing what was necessary in order to make him proud and to help save the world.

But Tikko hated the Hollywood scene, he was confident I had pursued it over him. He insisted I left on a jet plan for higher living years ago and hadn't looked back since. Truthfully, I had left—old ways, old schemes and old faults were all behind me. I wanted a better life, a tighter more legitimate family; one which was unified in accepting where we'd been but confident and poised for where we needed to go. More importantly, I wanted him to come with me—every hurdle, every pain and now with every new opportunity. But he didn't see my departures as opportunities. He saw them in the same way I had viewed my painful episodes in the past, as periods of isolation and distrust. He was alone with big responsibilities and little support.

Despite our back and forth quarrels around my comings and goings, time and experience had molded Tikko into a great father. He took pride in being the only man, most times the only *black* man at Saturday morning football games in Grain Valley and the Girl Scouts fall parade. When I was gone, he represented the two of us—an activity he cherished and made sure to tell all the neighborhood moms and dads about.

If there was one parenting proficiency we had not yet mastered, it was the skill of disciplining our children together, on one accord. He had been raised in a culture of spankings, threatening and lessons through punishment; me, well, I was a different story. Nothing really worked for mother, but I had learned enough from my village. I was determined to counsel through love and logic, provide positive reinforcements and enable my children with choices.

The discussion of how to blend our very dissimilar approaches became the source of many lively discussions, especially when I was away. One of the eldest children would call, "Dad is being mean . . . when are you coming home? I'm thinking of running away." I would explain how Dad's job was to be the parent—not the friend, and that structure is necessary to build respectful and responsible kids. I knew they didn't understand and how they longed for a little love and compassion amidst the endless constructive criticism. Although

I wasn't there I knew things were rocky and they showed no signs of getting better.

"Merideth, you can't always protect those kids," Tikko defended. ". . . that's the reason they don't want to do any work now, you always want to explain, have a conversation—I ain't got time for that."

We'd tussle back and forth as to why children must understand and be able to relate in a modern household. How, when empowered with choice and opportunity, they often choose the right road to take. He didn't get that, convinced of quite the opposite he contested the notion of reasoning with children, "I don't have to explain nothin' to no child . . . I refuse to argue. When I say do it—get it done, if not, it's yo' behind."

"But Tikko!" I'd shout in utter frustration, determined to win both the battle and the war. "You can't beat children for just anything. We'll never gain their respect through intimidation and fear."

Back and forth and back again.

Our only communication had resorted to arguments over how best to parent our kids.

But I knew the nature of our discussions had grown to much more than just talk when calls from the children became more frequent and progressively concerning. I was torn between them missing mom and the threat of parental abuse that might be going on. Both Tikko and I had spanked the children more than a time or two. But occasionally I peeked around corners, flinching in disagreement when I thought the tone of his voice was too strong or the number of belt lashings was one too many. Occasionally I'd step in, having heard enough, I was sure the kids needed my protection. Spanking might have been necessary, but I didn't like the place it was coming from. I had witnessed Tikko enraged so many times before. I was fearful and at times affirmed with direct witness, the emotion descending from his belt was wrath and not love.

Returning home one summer in August, after working three months in communities ravished by Hurricane Isaac, my worst fears were confirmed. A voicemail from a caseworker with Child Protective Services was my 'welcome home' greeting, an unwelcomed accusation forcing all prior parenting debates to cease. Now the state was involved and this wasn't the first time. A third "hotline" had been reported from anonymous sources, all different observers; they were concerned about the children's well-being and their safety around the only Dad they had ever known.

Tikko had become the source of a very serious charge. With Evan threatening to run away and Evelyn determined to take her own life, it would have been easy to pass off their threats as tirades of pubescent middle-schoolers; but the concerned tone in the caseworker's voice seemed to suggest not. When I returned her call the caseworker made it very clear—a decision needed to be made, it would be them or him. If I did nothing, the State would become involved.

She proceeded to explain the easiest, yet most aggressive way to remove Tikko from our home—an ex-porte, a restraining and protection order. Wow, here it was again, an opportunity to rid myself and the children of the unpredictable and sometimes frightening element that was Tikko. But could I really go through with it? He had grown so, evolved into a man who loved his family but fought hard, sometimes to the point of violence to defend and hold on to it. Was this fair, and would he perhaps leave on his own if he knew the decision I was being forced to make?

In my mind I couldn't muster up an assertive "absolutely!" I had tried to break us apart so many times before. I wanted to see if I could really live without Tikko, if I could tackle the task of real motherhood without him around to bail me out. I wanted to try. I knew separation even only for a brief period of time would be good for us, perhaps gratifying. He would come to know the value of self-worth, hard work and appreciate real love in all its many forms. Me, I hoped I would realize the value and the necessity of forgiveness and honesty, and that to love others to the point of intimacy requires I first love and adore God and then myself.

But he would never leave, despite the many times I tried and tried. He quickly countered, the thought of losing me even momentarily would be more than he could bear. He insisted he'd gone past the point of commitment. With so much of his time and his attention invested in our relationship, there was no possibility of separating or starting over. So there I was trapped in my own home, in a broken and perhaps distorted relationship. No room or space for my own identity outside of him.

And what about my babies? The threat of losing the children again came rushing back to memory. Immediately I broke out in a copious and frightened sweat. I couldn't breathe, I couldn't think straight. What was I going to do? The situation was much greater than what a few scatterbrained thoughts could muster up—this was serious. An intervention couldn't be avoided.

By this time in my continuum, I was daily evolving into a woman who panicked less and prayed more. After a word with my heavenly Father, asking only that His will be done, He gently guided me to seek counsel. I called the two strongest women I knew, mother and Christine. While their advice for the most part was the same: trust God, ask for discernment and leave as many people out of the decision for clarity-sake, their wisdom came from two very dissimilar places and from behind two starkly opposite perspectives.

To mother, I was her child—a woman scorned, robbed of her children during their youth and now reunited with them in grace. She wanted nothing of harm and bad fortune to come to anyone in the family, but especially not the children. She had fought for them, cried for them, fed, nurtured and sacrificed her very life for them. She helped purchase the home we built in Grain Valley, wanting all six of us to have a stable and safe environment in which to flourish and make things right. But she also loved Tikko and recognized perhaps this was an avenue in which he could seek help; help for his heart, his soul and his spirit of resentment. Perhaps he could come to terms with the chains of hurt, abandonment and substance abuse that for so long kept him from feeling whole.

From Christine's vantage point things were quite different. She knew me, she too loved the children and she'd come to know Tikko, he and definitely men his type. She herself had escaped from a man, literally packed up and left, when the physical, verbal and emotional abuse became too much for her to handle. She would recall a single moment, the breaking point in which she realized leaving was no longer optional, was when she put herself in her daughter's shoes and realized, more than a father or a father figure—her daughter needed her protection. She explained how she felt as she thought forward twenty-five years. Would her daughter grow up thinking this is how relationships ought to be, that it's ok for a man to beat the woman he loves?

She couldn't bear the thought of this being the legacy she left. As a mother, it was her divine and natural obligation to protect her child and herself. She paused just slightly to ensure I was still with her. With all the emotion of the last thirty-five years resounding in her voice she said, "Merideth, it is your job, your right to protect your children. You must protect the ones who cannot protect themselves. If Tikko needs help, allow him to get help . . . if God wills your marriage to be so, He will bring you two back together again."

I trekked in the street for hours, thinking, crying, even screaming out loud. The freight in my gut never lessoned when considering one move versus the other. But I closed my eyes, thanked God for what was to come and jumped. I chose the protection order, Tikko was served—I was nearby, watching fearfully from around the corner. I cried for hours after he was escorted from our home. I felt unsafe, guilty and deceitful all in the same sickening pit. I felt as though I had truly betrayed him; I was sure I had made a horrible mistake.

In the midst of our separation, a tremendous weight was lifted but a burden loomed just the same. As free as I was to move and make decisions without a co-signer, something was undoubtedly not ok. I fasted and prayed, holding closer than ever before to my collection of radio minsters and Christian music artists. Soon they became my daily dose of separation therapy. Listening to their ingenuously poignant lessons helped to strip the emotions from what I believed was a catastrophic situation and enabled me to focus more on the lesson to be learned inside the ever-evolving storm. It was a perfect storm in fact. Every other facet of my life had been touched, proven fixable by God . . . *Why not your marriage,* God suggested. I sneered, almost resented Him at the thought.

In the midst of the trial, I came to realize just how trying my own children had become. Perhaps the accusations against Tikko weren't fictitious, but I wondered if they had been exaggerated. I had been gone so long, but nevertheless I was sure I knew them well. All the children seemed to either have a moment of rebellion, engaging in complete anarchy now that Dad was gone, or Tikko was right; they were rambunctious and hard-headed and refused to listen to anyone for any reason. I feared the legitimacy of my decision even more. Mother stepped in as much as she could, an act of love but an apparent sacrifice. The kids were busy, needy and at times defiant. They took advantage of her presence and Tikko's absence in every way their little minds could conjure up. I struggled to revive my own love and logic approach and even found myself at times, reprimanding their defiant behaviors in octaves two and three scales too high.

I was determined to comply with the order, giving us all plenty of time and space to evoke healing, clarity and the possibility of change. The order of protection had become that in every sense of the word; it safeguarded Tikko and I from the selfish priorities that had so long caused our children to suffer. It restrained us from the damaging words, thoughts and actions we had let surface, some we kept hidden, and those that threatened to destroy our marriage all together. It would be a season of mercy if we wanted it to be, a time we could confess our hearts and faults to God if we chose. If we took advantage of the time away from one another and embraced the true meaning of sacrifice, we would find so much more outside of ourselves and our lack; we would discover the Christ that we *could be* to each other.

Occasionally Tikko and I spoke, but conversations remained short. He would call to express his disgust with my decision; I was puzzled how he could be so brash. Why didn't he realize my hands were tied, that an intervening action had to take place? Why was he so adamant I was to blame? Had I exaggerated the need for the intervention? Was I protecting my children the only way I knew how or manipulating the system as a way of escape. In my heart I was convicted it was a mixture of both, but I trusted the Lord to carry us through all the same.

Amidst all the chaos, mother was coping with her own season of testing. At ninety-six, Gran was dying; it wouldn't be long before the Lord called her home. For years Gran had persevered. Through her strength and the loving arms of God and His grace, she had been preserved and restored several times over, surviving segregation, poverty and the loss of so many loved ones—including her husband, her parents and each five one of her siblings.

At times I would gaze at her beautiful face in absolute amazement. During our final moments together I just sat and watched. With a divine peace she lay resting in her bed at the senior care facility that was now her home. Knowing not what to do or say, I caressed her fragile forearm and cold wrinkled hands, placing my head to hers. From the tear-soaked pillow I offered a soft rendition of *It is Well*, hoping it was truly well with her soul and that her mind was at rest. She opened her eyes, "We'll you look lovely today . . . ;" those would be her last words to me. I knew it was time, but in my world she would live forever. She was like Moses, radiating with the glory and goodness of God. She had been so faithful and obedient to the Lord throughout her lifetime; it was evident He was rewarding and daily keeping this His child.

She had overcome so many things in last few years—from bathroom falls to a mild stroke, it was as though she had graced death and then came running back. I like to believe her return each time was in hopes of preparing her eight children and countless grandchildren for her final departure from the earth.

She was a warrior, a sojourner for Christ. So many of us had come to the saving knowledge of Jesus because of the way she lived her life. She demonstrated true holiness, purity and a spirit of worship in every circumstance, even leading up to her final breaths. She would leave a legacy we could all strive to embody. She was a woman whose heart, voice and life craved and outwardly exuded the Lord. I would visit her as often as possible, singing the songs she so beautifully sang and stroking her silky white hair. She would sway her head and hum when she could muster the strength; I was so grateful for the moments we shared. I will carry these sweet, sweet treasures in my soul forever. Lying next to her, her heartbeat in perfect harmony with mine, I was sure I was experiencing the glory of Jesus himself. She knew my heart, she had overlooked my failures. I was forgiven in her eyes.

In the fall of 2012 as Hurricane Sandy bore relentlessly toward the eastern shore, I wondered how the pandemonium in my life at home would impact my ability to serve storm survivors in New York. With Tikko still gone, the kids would stay would mother. I hoped the extra company would help keep her mind stable if not totally at peace. As I kissed her and the children goodbye, I grabbed my suitcases packed with at least three months of home and riddled with emotions, and headed for the door. It was 4:33 am. The phone rang, Gran was gone. I turned in disbelief—sure the caller had dialed the wrong house. Mother in shock, she slumped into my waiting arms, "Moma's gone . . ." she wept, "My moma's gone . . ." I grabbed her to my chest, my own heart weeping inside. I stroked her hair just as I had stroked Gran's only days before. There we stood mourning the loss of our legacy. She was gone, resting peacefully in her Savior's loving arms.

———⟨❖⟩———

It still gives me chills to recall the events around Gran's passing. It was scene out of a Hollywood movie: Jesus intervenes with a sudden phone call right as I reach for the knob of the front door. His timing is always perfect because His ways are not our ways; His thoughts exceed far beyond what our limited, carnal minds can comprehend. He knows what we need and is faithful to provide it, many times whether we ask for His interference or not. He knew mother would need an anchor, a shoulder and an able mind to process rational, orderly thoughts. He knew an immediate grief would engulf mother before a spirit of praise, so He sent me. Riddled with my own selfish thoughts and circumstances Jesus nudged, "Ok Merideth, it's your time to serve, lay aside your own consuming weights, your mother needs *you* now."

Together we made the trip to Gran's funeral, a six hundred-mile drive to Winnsboro, Louisiana. On board were passengers from three generations: mother, daughter and grandchildren. The homecoming was a celebration in every right, people from all over the country descended on the little town of just under 5,000 residents to honor the life of our beloved matriarch. Two unexpected guests had come to be with me; another part of God's plan, the healing along my life's continuum I'm sure. My father Pete—a lifelong resident of Winnsboro, and my sister Faye, a woman I had never met before, were there to be the comforting anchors for me. I don't know why, but I thanked God the two of them were there.

I'm not sure what it was, perhaps the emotion of a great loss or maybe a heart ripened and soft. Perhaps God had been preparing me for this moment all along and He knew this was the time, the place where forgiveness and restoration would be found. I'll never forget how mother crept into my hotel room, clearly struggling for the words to tell me my father had just arrived. She cautioned him, "I'm not sure what she'll do Pete, what she'll say . . . we'll just have to see how it goes."

At first I laughed and then realized who he was. This was my father, the giver of my life and he wanted me—to kiss, hug and love me; I was his daughter. As

121

if I was a schoolgirl who had skinned her knee on the gravel playground and wanted her daddy to make it better, years of strife and bitterness melted away and I went running to greet my father. Lifelong connections were made, tears were shed, emails and phone numbers exchanged. It was as though we'd never been apart—a father and his two daughters. Somehow I felt whole, I finally felt like I belonged.

As we made the long drive home, duty called again; it was time to serve those who needed support and a source of hope the most. Hurricane Sandy had hit the northeastern states head on. This time, I was ready and eager to go. Gathering my thoughts and compiling a last-minute list of things to do, I thanked God for this place to which I had come. Loose ends had been tied, a broken heart was being mended, and I was so grateful to have survived.

I realized in that moment what God had been preparing me for over the span of a lifetime, the purpose He planned all along. I was chosen to serve, to teach and to minister. It wasn't me, but my story that could possibly change the world. Through my testimony I could attest how God rescued me from a life of sin and destruction. I could explain how by His grace I was spared at times when I least deserved it, all for the purpose of giving Him the glory; in my life He would have center stage. This life was never about me, but the work God had ordained me to do. I understood and I embraced this truth, it was His truth and His omniscient power now revealed.

> For I know the plans I have for you," declares the Lord, "plans to prosper you and not to harm you, plans to give you hope and a future. (Jeremiah 29:11)

Three days into my deployment for Hurricane Sandy I found myself tackling one of the biggest challenges of my life. The girl who was once isolated from the rest of the team was now managing one of the largest masses of disaster aid respondents. Over thirteen hundred to be exact—organize them, coordinate their movement and supplies, and dispatch them across the entire state of New York where Sandy had left its devastating mark.

Years ago I would have touted the opportunity as an unprecedented chance to shine. But that wasn't me anymore, with self being much further down the priority list I knew God had placed me there for two very simple reasons: to minister and to serve. Although Christ was not physically at the head of the bigger man-led operation, I was determined to make Him the head of mine. He was the silent guest at every team meeting, behind the words of every memo and every strategic plan. I knew if I sought Him first, embracing the traits of a Christ-like leader, He would take charge, go before and alongside me; lives would be forever impacted, both the staff's and the hurricane survivors we served.

God did amazing things there in New York. Together we met a lot of special people along the way. One in particular would leave a lasting impression; she would reaffirm the surreal nature and expansive depth of God's emerging plan.

I met Reverend Dr. Cheryl Anthony when her community had been devastated by the destruction Sandy left behind. She was much like my Gran, a sojourner, an advocate for her constituents and for Christ. She toiled sun up to sun down, so much so she didn't even stop to celebrate Thanksgiving with her family. Instead she, her family and the members of her small Brooklyn church brought Thanksgiving to others as they served meals, delivered clothes and gave hope to those who had lost everything. After a couple of meetings, I realized she was a servant after God's own heart. "One day," I thought, "I'm going to be like her." Her tireless efforts were amazing to watch, I was captivated by the way she inspired and forever impacted each life she touched.

Reverend Anthony was an amazing woman who spoke little of her many accomplishments and accolades. Serving on councils for past Presidents and fostering policies on minority health, equality and professional advancement, she was a woman who had been no doubt rewarded for her faithful service to one powerful God.

Together we braved the ravished streets and homes of Coney Island. Arm in arm with food, information and as many resources as we could muster, we battled so many elements—from naysayers to the bitter cold. We stopped at nothing to reach as many people as time, physical strength and daylight would afford.

The night before I was to return home to attend a mandatory court hearing on the children's protection order, Reverend Anthony looking directly into the corners of my heart, advised from the second floor of her brownstone church,

"Merideth hunie, don't be afraid to walk in God's will for your life. Trust Him in everything you do. You are an anointed woman of God and He has placed you here, in this place for His appointed purpose, for such a season . . . for such a time as this."

Her words shook me to the core. I couldn't help but think they were so familiar and had graced my ears from a pulpit somewhere, some years before. But I couldn't remember. I wanted to recall the story; I needed to know what *time* she was referring to. Her words were so powerful and rightfully so; I soon found they stemmed directly from the Word of God.

The scripture she referenced came from the Old Testament story of Esther. An orphan raised by her cousin Mordecai, Esther was chosen by King Ahasuerus of Susa to be his queen, a decision made in order to replace the recalcitrant Queen Vashti who refused to appear before the King and his guests in a very personal exhibition of her beauty.

Mordecai was a trusted friend of both King Ahasuerus and now Queen Esther. Esther 2:21-23 describes how on one occasion when Mordecai was sitting at the king's gates, he overheard two of the king's officers plotting to assassinate the king. Mordecai informed Esther of the plot, who then warned the king. Mordecai was lauded for his loyalty to the king and his wise counsel to his surrogate daughter.

Later in the story, King Ahasuerus granted Haman, a prominent Agagite prince, special honors. Part of this endowment required all the people to bow down to Haman as he traveled throughout the city streets. Esther 3:1-4 describes how all but Mordecai, a Jew, complied. Mordecai stood firm on his position, insisting he will bow to no one but God. Enraged by Mordecai's insubordination, Haman together with his wife and advisors plotted against the Jews, devising a plan to kill and essentially extinguish all Jews throughout the Persian Empire; a plan that would have prompted the first recorded holocaust against Jewish people. After bringing charges of treason against the Jews, Haman gained the king's approval to initiate the plan; sealing it by decree and ten thousand silver talents.

In an outward display of grief and mourning, Mordecai tore his robes and put ashes on his head upon hearing the news. Despite Esther's efforts to console,

Mordecai remained with torment. He explained to Esther if she did nothing, God's plan would include the deliverance of his people through another source and she would indeed be killed if she didn't do whatever she could to stop the massacre; this meant intervening on behalf of the Jews. Esther would have to talk to the king.

Customary in those times, Esther was not permitted to see the king unless he called for her. Approaching the king could result in certain death. Esther loved God and her people, especially Mordecai. Her yearning to be faithful to her family and her faith, all the while tempering a mounting sense of terror, brought Esther to a crossroads.

As Esther wrestled with the reality before her, Mordecai proved to be a trusted friend and a sound presence facilitating the word and will of God. In Esther 4:14b he says,

> . . . And who knows but that you have come to your royal position
> for such a time as this?

After earnestly fasting and praying for three days, Esther found peace in her decision to obey God, she would approach the King and her people would be saved.

Wow. Did you see that? God had orchestrated Esther's rearing as a child, her position and her rise to prominence, for a very distinct time, place and purpose. God would demonstrate His power and complete authority as God through one very common and unsuspecting woman in a very uncommon and miraculous way.

Like Esther, I found myself in a relentless season, a year of painstaking trials. Just as Esther believed Mordecai, I believed Reverend Anthony and I believed the promises of God. If He could do the unthinkable for Mordecai, Esther, and this small but mighty woman from Brooklyn, New York, He could do the impossible for me as well, beyond anything I could ask or think.

When I returned I was confident, almost certain how the court hearing would turn out. A guardian ad litem had been appointed by the court to represent the children in the midst of our separation. Her job was to be the fact-finder and to ensure before the protection order was lifted, both mother and father had the children's best interest at heart. She spoke with Tikko and me on many occasions prior, just to see where our heads were at; how discipline was really being handled, would the children be returning to a safe and nurturing environment, and could the two of us recover as husband and wife.

After numerous conversations Tikko and I came to the conclusion that between the two of us, there was still work to be done. I wasn't convinced he had used his time away as I had hoped—seeking God, listening for a revelation, but then again, those weren't my choices to make. I knew one thing to be true, he desperately missed his children and without them he realized his life wasn't whole. I rejoiced in his discovery but deeply wanted him to experience so much more. On many occasions I tried to explain the unexplainable love and peace of Jesus Christ. I described how he would never find real joy in pursuing me, a life of wealth or even a life pain-free; only God could fill him with a supernatural euphoria that would never subside.

Through our distance I learned to appreciate the man and the caregiver Tikko had become. I realized for far too long I was resentful, at times purposely punishing him. I didn't recognize just how far he had traveled to evolve into the man I wanted him to be. Regardless if he walked with Jesus or not, he was my husband and it was my biblical responsibility to be a light, an example for his life—to love him, to encourage him and to forgive him, just as I had been forgiven by Christ.

The morning of the court hearing we felt good, like children racing to the family room to unwrap presents on Christmas morning—we were on our way downtown . . . to get our family back. We were greeted by the guardian ad litem when we arrived, she explained a few administrative details—appear before the judge, a few questions, a few answers and we'd be on our way. Her recommendation was solid, the order would be dropped and we would leave as parents—father and mother together again. I was giddy inside, I felt myself say, "This is going to work; we're going to do it this time . . . we're finally on the same page."

When our case was called, the questions began. Soon, questions became interrogation. Wait, wasn't I the victim here? I was sure I was dreaming. The guardian ad litem had me in her sights, her calm reassuring nature just minutes before had shifted into that of a raging bull spitting darts of fire . . .

"And is it true Mrs. Parrish that you only used the protection order as a measure of intervention . . ."

"Yes . . . but . . ." I tried to explain.

"And did you ever witness the Respondent, Tikko Parrish physically abuse or bring harm to the children?" she probed like some crazed character out of *CSI*.

"I did in fact witness numerous occasions in which I thought the discipline had gone too far . . ."

Refuting any truth I attempted to contend with, her questioning to Mr. Parrish went quite the opposite.

"Mr. Parrish, so when the Petitioner Mrs. Parrish was gallivanting away on deployments attempting to save the world, who was principally responsible for caring for all four children?"

"I was, ma'am" he said almost immediately. He said nothing more.

Her questions of Tikko continued only a few brief moments longer. They were assumptive, almost jovial even; she clearly believed I was to blame.

She proceeded to tell the judge she was appalled by my exploitation of a very serious and already overwhelmed judicial system. She insisted I be held liable for perjury and for clearly embellishing charges of parental abuse.

I froze in horror, eyes blurred by the uncontrollable rush of tears. I couldn't believe what I was hearing. I prayed the judge would probe a little more, ask more open-ended questions and give me a chance to paint a more accurate story. Perhaps he understood where I was coming from and had closely studied my claims. I hoped he knew I was a domestic violence survivor and he would reprimand Tikko for failing to keep his temper and his emotions under control, even now years later.

But he didn't, in fact he attacked with much greater vigor than she. He was determined to make an example out of me, his voice grew in volume and my opportunity to speak was no more. I could only gaze like a buck ensnared with fear as he continued in a tyrannical rage,

"As a federal government employee you ought to be ashamed of yourself . . . you have given this court and this entire process a bad name. It's women like you who abuse the system, you use it to your advantage."

By this time I was sure I had stopped breathing . . .

"You clutter up our dockets to prove a point—perform an 'intervention' as you call it with your boyfriends and husbands, while women who really need help are getting their heads bashed in . . . don't you come into my court getting all matter of fact with me, you better be glad I'm not pressing criminal charges for your willful perjury."

In one last valiant effort, I attempted to revive the memory of our violent past. But in one fell swoop he summoned me silent. His judgment was rendered: the protection order released and a lofty fine to teach me a lesson.

Keeping my composure as long as I could, I ran out of the courtroom full of tears and humiliation. The ordeal was over, but I wasn't sure what had just happened. After an hour-long cry session over the phone with mother, Tikko and I headed home.

Five days after Tikko returned home as husband and father, I returned to my ongoing deployment in New York. Feeling as though a burden had been lifted I marveled in the miracles God continued to perform. Each new challenge produced another "Thank You Jesus" or a new song lauding the Savior's keeping power; I was fully walking in His grace. This was a season of great clarity and purpose. I was crafting my life's story in hopes of sharing it with the world.

Days and nights leading disaster recovery operations for Hurricane Sandy were grueling, emotional, and sometimes heartbreaking. Weeks no longer consisted of days but hours that seemingly ran together; we only noticed it was dawn by the rush of commuters who crowded the subways and grimy New York streets every morning during rush hour. Many nights we toiled into the early hours, skipping meals, surviving only on coffee and mints, oftentimes bunking in a co-worker's room when we just didn't have the strength to make it to our own hotel door.

Hurricane Sandy was a big operation, drawing thousands of federal, non-profit, private sector and faith-based volunteers and workers to help those whose lives had been destroyed in a matter of days. On many occasions the sights and smells of the ravished boroughs and already impoverished neighborhoods were more than the stomach and spirit could handle. I cried myself to sleep many nights, overwhelmed by sheer exhaustion and a momentary sense of hopelessness—realizing we just could reach everyone, and wouldn't possibly be able to make every survivor whole again. On those nights, it was only the grace and power of Jesus that sustained me. It's an awesome, surreal power that simply cannot be described in words. It's a power manifested through the Holy Spirit living inside me which knows, when I have just enough energy and strength to say, "Jesus," God hears me, He knows my need and He answers me. And on other nights that power was the miraculous protection that occurred when I stumbled into my hotel room at 4am, clothes and shoes still on, collapsing on the bed and drifting off to sleep. Many nights I even forgot to close and the lock door behind me. This was God.

You see, the great thing about God (amount countless other things) is that He is a God after our own hearts. Nothing pleases Him more than to love and care for His children. He is equally pleased when His children love, obey and follow after Him. In His concern, He affords His protection, His guidance and His strength—through the Father, the Son and the Holy Spirit. He also gives us companions, great friends. Many times friends are the greatest gifts, tangible resources we have to survive the seasons we often find ourselves traveling through. In my New York season, Andrea was undoubtedly, the greatest gift the Father provided to enable me to survive the storm—literally.

Andrea was one of the women of faith I met during my first field experience in Columbia years prior. She was the modern-day equivalent to a beautiful, faithful woman of God found in the Bible known as Ruth. Like Ruth, Andrea was very quiet, a kindred spirit and a gentle creature who knew and loved the Word. She also loved people and was faithful to her mission of caring for each person as though they were her own child. Feeding people, hugging people and making them smile—Andrea went out of her way to ensure people knew they were loved. I loved her spirit and I bathed in her light, it was contagious. To some people it was annoying, but I loved it.

Months prior in our working together we would bond, form an unwritten and unspoken pact to exhibit the love and gospel of Jesus Christ everywhere we went. Together our conversations, our dealings with people and the manner in which we handled ourselves would embody the Word of God, intentionally so. It wasn't our effort to be haughty or demonstrate our superior Christian values, but to capitalize on an opportunity, a true mission field-based work that came with each new disaster. Tornadoes, floods and hurricanes were destructive and calamitous, but we would count it all joy, considering each new opportunity a privilege to deliver the love and light of Jesus Christ.

I survived many days in New York simply because of the Christ-like love shown by Andrea. On days when exhaustion threatened to render me ill, she prayed. When hunger and deliriousness overtook me and I refused to stop working just for a moment to refuel, she fed me. And each morning, each and every morning before we started our workday, Andrea arrived to the office early before everyone else arrived, taking the time to pray, find a Bible verse to encourage and empower me, and post it ever so subtly on a Post-It note on the upper left-hand corner of my computer screen. I often found myself marveling at her ability to demonstrate true, unfiltered Godly love. If she hurt, if she was tired, if she was hungry, you never knew it. She served simply for the love of serving. She toiled without reward and hated when people took notice. But I noticed. Returning the favors with lunch and Starbucks™ coffee whenever I could, I noticed.

The capstone of my journey occurred during one of our final team meetings. It was amidst one of our most taxing periods; confidence was shaken, people were tired and faces were long. When the Holy Spirit prompted so vividly and unexpectedly, I paused and asked my staff, "Does anyone mind if we pray?" I couldn't deny the cloud of Godly protection and materialized grace that had covered our work all this time. I thanked the Lord for another revelation and for giving me the courage to be obedient to His commands. While perhaps there were many faiths, many different continuums and conditions of people in the room that day, I know lives and hearts were changed. I praised God for using me to be a light to a great company of strangers and rejoiced in knowing their lives would never be the same.

When it was time for me to depart for good, I was humbled by the team's expressions of love and gratitude. Among the table of food, gifts and cards was a table of tribute—select bible verses the team had collected from my personal wall of inspiration (Andrea's daily Bible Post-Its) atop my office desk. I smiled with sincere humility, searching for the appropriate words to say. I looked at Andrea. She smiled and I cried, whispering softly through an emotional whimper,

"This is what it's all about, I finally understand. If we accomplish nothing else here in New York, this table here confirms we've done what the Lord called us to do. God is in this place no doubt, God is in this place."

Chapter 11

Embracing the "We" God Made Us to Be

So now you know my story—all the missteps, the victories, the terrors and the tests. The best part of this non-fiction fable? It's not over; God is still busy at work and because of His matchless grace, I survived. From birth my life was cultivated by a village of Christ-followers and in some cases strangers ordained by God's design. Supported by their never-ending love, discipline and nurturing care I traveled along my continuum fulfilling a unique and special purpose, one created for every aspect of my life, including this very moment in time.

By now I've bumped my head so many times it's grown an extra layer of skin as a defense mechanism. I've taken risks and I've been wounded to the core. All in all, I've learned so many invaluable lessons that have equipped me to look past the overwhelming appearance of life's intricacies and focus keenly on the capacity of Jesus Christ. God is a supernatural being with supernatural power, that's what makes Him God. We simply cannot fathom with our mortal and feeble minds, what He is capable of doing on our behalf. This life, by its sinful nature is corrupt and in need of a hero—a supernatural hero. When we realize it is impossible to live, thrive and succeed without Christ, we can all make greater strides along our own continuums.

When I started this journey it was always my goal to capture my story for someone else—the mother who was desperate for answers, the wife who was trapped in an abusive relationship, the child whose parent wasn't a parent at all, or the husband who felt so disconnected from his family. God quickly revealed this journey was willed for much more than ministering to the masses. It would be the vehicle through which I would learn who I was and now, who I am. It would reveal the inhibitors that for so long have kept me from living and how I must learn to forgive and move forward if I want to thrive and exist with purpose. And it would write the words to a brand new love song, the most beautiful song known to man—a message of how God wanted more than anything to restore us back to Himself. He gave us life, opportunities, a faithful family, good friends and not to mention free will. But above all these, He demonstrated the meaning of true love by granting us His forgiveness. In the end, He himself would be the ultimate sacrifice. For everything we were not and could never be, He gave us a second chance, the hope of eternal life.

Perhaps this story has helped me more than it has helped you. But it is my prayer as you travel along your own continuum, you've reflected on the pieces of your life and pondered how you yourself are coming along. Before you can acknowledge where you are in your journey and the projected path to your future, you must first embrace who you are in Christ and His intended purpose for your life.

For me it was important to first reflect on my past as it revealed everything and every person I was not. Not knowing who I really was or who I was designed to be caused me to adopt behaviors and accept lifestyles related to any and everything; a complete contradiction to God's deliberate design. Of course I had the choice of how I wanted to live and the real-life character I would portray, but how effective is an actor without a script, or a science teacher without his science book? Without a foundation rooted in God's Word, I had no visibility of God's expectations for my life and the specific functions He wanted me to carry out. I was living life blindly, without direction and no clear indication of course. And by failing to pause momentarily—to evaluate my steps and get realigned with God's mission—I strayed further and further away from His designated plan.

Over the course of my journey I've fallen in love with so many parts of God's word. When I'm concerned about how something's going to turn out, I read Psalms 89 and Isaiah 26 which describe the greatness of God's awesome power. John 14 is especially timely when I struggle to let go of painful memories and feelings of betrayal. And whenever I need to be reassured of just how much I am loved by my Father, I turn to 1 Corinthians and Romans 8. Undoubtedly there are countless places in the Bible where we can see how much we mean to God and how His greatest desire is for us to serve and worship Him in every aspect of our lives.

No matter where you are along your continuum, choosing Christ means you acknowledge and embrace the truth that Christ has chosen you. What an amazing thing to be chosen, for life and for redemption—Wow, you were chosen for God's kingdom!

Knowing the real you can help empower your life. When blessed with the *knowledge* and the *truth* as to who you are in Christ, you can be totally *honest* with yourself—about your limitations, God's supernatural power to aid you despite those limitations, and the direction in which you should go, now and every day to come.

Knowing who you are in Christ comes only by knowing the Word. Yep, you got it—God has an app for that. If you do nothing else after reading my story, read the book of Ephesians. I love everything about this book as it outlines so clearly and beautifully the "we" God created us to be. Yes, God did an amazing thing by crafting a supernatural plan of redemption, a plan to restore His fallen, most prized creation (human beings) back to himself and to His heart. God created man in his image—to be flawless beings; our perfection a mark of His absolute power, an outward demonstration of His holiness as God. In addition to this perfect plan, He imparted a piece of himself inside each one of us. He gave us his Holy Spirit equipped with the functions we need to live, forgive, love others, invoke healing and to serve. To understand the spirit of God that dwells in you is to understand the "Me" He created you to be. In order to find peace, the kind that only God can give, you must learn to embrace those things that are of God's spirit; only then will true change come. When you know and understand the spirit of God, you have answered the question, 'God Who?'

If you're still struggling to understand who God is and how to incorporate His spirit, His teachings and His will into your life, I challenge you to do these four things:

1) Learn to Embrace a "True Love" that is Godly Love

We've all claimed it at one time or another, "I'm in love . . . he's definitely the one." As human beings, it's important for us to realize the only way we can know "true love" or ever hope to experience such a phenomenal condition, is through the love of the Father; the love God gives us as His children.

Ephesians chapter 2 describes this absolute, unconditional love,

> [4] *But because of his great love for us, God, who is rich in mercy,* [5] *made us alive with Christ even when we were dead in transgressions—it is by grace you have been saved.*

> [10] *For we are God's masterpiece. He has created us anew in Christ Jesus, so that we can do the good things he planned for us long ago.*

And because God possesses such an infinite love, He himself is love. He is not a God of hate, hateful things or a hateful nature. Remember, we were created in the image of God hence we were designed with the same spirit of love which comprises God himself. Because God is love, He expects us to love others,

> [34] *A new command I give you: Love one another. As I have loved you, so you must love one another.* [35] *By this everyone will know that you are my disciples, if you love one another. (John 13:34-35)*

What does this mean for you and I? God loved us and will forever love us in a way that no man ever will. People will betray us, hurt our feelings and no doubt even break our hearts. But once we understand how much we are loved by God, we can appreciate just how precious all people are—even those we can't imagine loving at all. Love changes the way we view the things people do and the way in which we respond to certain behaviors. Love will take the most bitter of memories, the most hurtful of words and dissolve them into mere vapor. Love looks beyond the faults of our family, friends, children and spouses and embraces them as people, reflections of God's heart. It helps us see beyond what we believe they are not, and celebrate them for who and what they are.

God loved me so much He gave me two mothers, a father and a village of families to nurture me throughout my life. He established an environment in which I could learn and hear the gospel, and even covered me with a cloud of grace when I blazed off to unearth a life I thought I was missing. He loved my children, especially Evan and Evelyn; He protected them countless nights when I left them behind. And He loved Tikko and I both, despite how we sorely denied Him and grieved His heart unjustifiably so. Over time I have come to realize only a God, Jesus Christ could love like this. I am so grateful for this love and because I now know it well, the journey along the rest of my continuum will never be the same.

2) Dare to Embrace a Forgiveness like the Father's

In order to walk in the "you" God destined, you must almost embrace a spirit of forgiveness. Forgiving those who have hurt you, particularly those who have destroyed the very roots of your joy, could quite possibly be one of the most difficult challenges of your life. But with Christ living inside you, the spirit of God radiating throughout, forgiveness is possible. You too without question can live and thrive in the freedom and healing that comes when you forgive.

How is this possible? Christ forgave us, hence we are not only capable, but we are supernaturally empowered to forgive others. Here's what Ephesians chapter 2 says,

> [6] *And God raised us up with Christ and seated us with him in the heavenly realms in Christ Jesus,* [7] *in order that in the coming ages he might show the incomparable riches of his grace, expressed in his kindness to us in Christ Jesus.*
>
> [8] ***For it is by grace you have been saved***, *through faith—and this is not from yourselves, it is the gift of God—* [9] *not by works, so that no one can boast.*
>
> —[12] *remember that at that time you were separate from Christ, excluded from citizenship in Israel and foreigners to the covenants of the promise, without hope and without God in the world.* [13] *But now in Christ Jesus you who once were far away have been brought near by the blood of Christ.*
>
> [14] *For he himself is our peace, who has made the two groups one and has destroyed the barrier, the dividing wall of hostility,* [15] *by setting aside in his flesh the law with its commands and regulations. His purpose was to create in himself one new humanity out of the two, thus making peace,* [16] *and in one body to reconcile both of them to God through the cross, by which he put to death their hostility.*

¹⁹ Consequently, you are no longer foreigners and strangers, but fellow citizens with God's people and also members of his household, ²⁰ built on the foundation of the apostles and prophets, with Christ Jesus himself as the chief cornerstone.

The Bible's justification for forgiveness couldn't be clearer. We were in need of a Savior. As a means of physical, spiritual and eternal intervention, God offered Jesus Christ as the sacrificial lamb to come to our rescue.

God had every right to wipe me off the face of the earth when I chose to reject His instructions and His will for my life. But He didn't. He whispered my name, dispatched a few angles and waited patiently for me to return back to Him again. He didn't have to give me time and space to run, but He did—I'm so thankful He did.

For years I hated Tikko, the older boys at my church who touched me inappropriately and my father who watched me grow from a distance, but didn't bother to write. But it was the pain of unforgiveness that was causing me to suffer; my own selfishness and self-pride was destroying me—emotionally, mentally, spiritually and physically. I couldn't forgive myself for leaving my babies so I ate my way to over 250 pounds and attempted to recover lost time with countless presents and expensive toys. I harbored unforgiveness against my former boss who left me in the field so long. For months I hampered myself and my own professional advancement because I couldn't see past my ego and the severity of his wrongs.

Once I started to forgive, I felt years of weight giving way to peace. Like all things along my continuum, learning to forgive has been a process; it's a spirit of being I ask God to empower me with daily. And every day He grants, through opportunity or a quick jaunt through painful memories, giving me the chance to be forgiving and to love others unconditionally, just as He loved and forgave me.

3)   Choose to be Fulfilled through an Unwavering Faith

I'm sure at one point in your life you've come across Hebrews 11:1; if not the verse, the text that follows: "Now faith is the substance of things hoped for, the evidence of things not seen." But have you ever thought about what this really means? Simply put, faith is what happens when trust and truth collide. Remember, truth represents the conditions we know to be factual, guaranteed to take place. You'll also remember that there are certain truths about God, who He is, what He has done and what He plans to do; things like He's a holy God incapable of sin, He was crucified and resurrected to save us from eternal damnation, and in His pure and perfect nature, He cannot tell a lie. These are truths.

The trust we place in the authenticity and the materialization of these truths is our faith. We need look no further than the miracles performed at Christ's hand and the earthly manifestations of Biblical prophesies to know there is truth in the Trinity we worship. Not only is our faith the foundation and confirmation of what we believe, but it should also be the sole source of human fulfillment, the framework by which we live out our entire lives.

What do you mean Merideth? Here are some truths:

You were made to live!

The thief comes only to steal and kill and destroy; I have come that they may have life, and have it to the full. (John 10:10)

> **Truth:** The devil will do anything he can to ensure we jeopardize and completely obliterate our chances of being reunited with Christ. To be reunited means to have eternal life. Jesus Christ came to earth, died and rose—permanently defeating the devil and his reign over us. This doesn't mean however, the devil's going to let up anytime soon. Jesus came to give us life—beyond what we could ever imagine, both here on earth and eternally with Him in heaven.

> **How Can I be Fulfilled through Faith?** Knowing this truth, you can refute and resist every trick of the devil, every lie and deception he attempts to claim for your life. Realize, God wants to empower you with life—an amazing, healthy, prosperous life. Trust and know that God has done the impossible; he has defeated death to

bring you life. Ahh, that's it, let out a sigh of relief. You're in God's hands.

Live as Unto the Lord!

[15] Be very careful, then, how you live—not as unwise but as wise, [16] making the most of every opportunity, because the days are evil. [17] Therefore do not be foolish, but understand what the Lord's will is. [18] Do not get drunk on wine, which leads to debauchery. Instead, be filled with the Spirit. (Ephesians 5:15-18)

[20] That, however, is not the way of life you learned [21] when you heard about Christ and were taught in him in accordance with the truth that is in Jesus. [22] You were taught, with regard to your former way of life, to put off your old self, which is being corrupted by its deceitful desires; [23] to be made new in the attitude of your minds; [24] and to put on the new self, created to be like God in true righteousness and holiness. (Ephesians 4:20-24)

[8] For you were once darkness, but now you are light in the Lord. Live as children of light [9] (for the fruit of the light consists in all goodness, righteousness and truth) [10] and find out what pleases the Lord. (Ephesians 5:8-10)

> **Truth:** God has proven faithful countless times; just look at my story. Even when I least deserved it, He outfitted me with His covering and His grace. When I chose to rebel and resist His calling, I suffered, encountered hardships that by myself I was ill-equipped to handle and I made some decisions that nearly cost me my life. Needless to say, by myself in the absence of Christ, I am nothing.
>
> **How Can I be Fulfilled through Faith?** Like a caterpillar sheds its cocoon once it has transformed into its beautiful butterfly state, we as children of God must embrace the *Brand New Funkier "Me's"* God intended us to be. With confidence (and a supernatural faith) we can feel good walking in the image and likeness of God. Serving the Lord

requires us to sacrifice ourselves and pursue those activities that wholly worship and please Him, both in spirit and in truth. If we want to experience real fulfillment—a joy that only Christ can give—we must live a life that's pleasing and acceptable to God.

The Armor that Can't be Defeated

[10] Finally, be strong in the Lord and in his mighty power. [11] Put on the full armor of God, so that you can take your stand against the devil's schemes.

[12] For our struggle is not against flesh and blood, but against the rulers, against the authorities, against the powers of this dark world and against the spiritual forces of evil in the heavenly realms. [13] Therefore put on the full armor of God, so that when the day of evil comes, you may be able to stand your ground, and after you have done everything, to stand.

[14] Stand firm then, with the belt of truth buckled around your waist, with the breastplate of righteousness in place, [15] and with your feet fitted with the readiness that comes from the gospel of peace. [16] In addition to all this, take up the shield of faith, with which you can extinguish all the flaming arrows of the evil one. [17] Take the helmet of salvation and the sword of the Spirit, which is the word of God. (Ephesians 6:10-17)

> **Truth:** No battle, no weapon, no earthly snare is too powerful for our God. If we ask anything of God with unwavering faith, He will hear our prayers and meet our needs according to His will. He will battle to the death and beyond for His children; there's nothing our God cannot do. Without God's covering we leave ourselves open, vulnerable and exposed. God himself has created the appropriate defense to ensure nothing can penetrate us if we are obedient to His Word.

How Can I be Fulfilled through Faith? Doesn't it feel good to know God's got your back? Trust Him, believe his many promises for you and your journey. Entrench yourself in the full armor of God and prepare to be amazed by the mighty works He does in your life.

4)   Boldly Embrace the Call to *Know* God

There's nothing more rewarding than knowing you can come back home. Jesus said, "The door is open . . ." He's waiting, longing for you to come in. If you haven't accepted Jesus Christ as your Lord and personal Savior, I would be wrong not to tell you why you should. Life is too short to spend it "playing church" or to guess what will happen once your body leaves this earth. I would hate for you to be the one forced to open that shiny gold box.

At one time I was so uncertain; I was sure I had done too much, gone too far to be forgiven by God. But I was wrong and I chose to believe Jesus. I dared Him to carry out His promises. And He did just that, day after day. He sent loving reminders through the bright sunshine and a soft caress through a gentle wind. Every time a twinge of doubt would arise, He sent me something or someone to reaffirm I was His.

So I closed my eyes and raised my arms in a motion of surrender as He gently whispered, "Fall away Merideth, fall away." I fell back and He caught me, He's carrying me still. My life will never be the same.

If you don't know the Lord, but in your heart you are convinced you are ready to meet Him, love Him and truly know Him, pray this simple prayer with me,

> *Lord, as I'm traveling along my life's continuum, I've realized I don't know you as well as I should. I've asked myself the question 'God Who?' and now realize I don't quite have all the answers. I'd like to change that starting today; I want to be one with you.*

> *I admit I am a sinner and that my sins separate me from you. Please forgive me, I repent of my sins and turn away from my sinful past.*

I believe you, Jesus Christ are the true Son of God. I believe you died on a cross for my sins, were raised from the dead by God the Father on the third day, and are now alive, hearing and answering my prayers.

I believe the blood you shed on the cross has washed away my sins. And I believe one day you are coming back for your children; I want to be one of them. Today, I'm asking you Jesus to become my Savior and the Lord of my life. I surrender myself to you totally and completely, I am yours from this day forward.

Please send me your Holy Spirit so I can be more like you. Please increase your spirit within me so that I am convicted when I sin and will continue to grow in the grace and knowledge of you.

I pledge from this moment on to be a light to the rest of the world, a light proclaiming the good news of salvation and my commitment to follow you for the rest of my life.

In Jesus' name I pray, Amen.

And it is written,

[9] At this, those who heard began to go away one at a time, the older ones first, until only Jesus was left, with the woman still standing there. [10] Jesus straightened up and asked her,

"Woman, where are they? Has no one condemned you?"

[11] "No one, sir," she said.

"Then neither do I condemn you," Jesus declared.

"Go now and leave your life of sin."(John 8:9-11)

Welcome to Christ's family. May your life be forever changed as you continue along your *continuum of Christian character.*

About the Author

Merideth Parrish is a notable blogger in the social media scene, writing about personal and thought-provoking topics drawn from her own experiences. A graduate of Park University's Hauptmann School for Public Affairs, Parrish works as a public affairs professional for a federal agency and is an adjunct professor for communications for a local university. She lives with her husband, her four children, and her five felines in Grain Valley, Missouri.

Made in the USA
Lexington, KY
21 December 2013